peta heskell

THE FLIRT COACH'S GUIDE TO FINDING THE LOVE YOU WANT

communication tips for
relationship success

element

To PNB for teaching me that when you stop planning and go with the flow, life can become an exciting adventure. Thanks for being a great friend, lover and fellow adventurer.

Element
An Imprint of HarperCollins*Publishers*
77–85 Fulham Palace Road
Hammersmith, London W6 8JB

The website address is: www.thorsonselement.com

 ™

and *Element* are trademarks of
HarperCollins*Publishers* Ltd

Published by Element 2003

10 9 8 7 6 5 4 3 2 1

© Peta Heskell 2003

Peta Heskell asserts the moral right to be
identified as the author of this work

A catalogue record of this book is
available from the British Library

ISBN 0 00 714767 8

Printed and bound in Great Britain by
Martins The Printers Ltd, Berwick upon Tweed

CONTENTS

ACKNOWLEDGEMENTS

A huge thank you to all my friends, including the Goddesses and the South Coast girlies – you know who you are – for so freely sharing your lives and loves with me and for helping me through my own trials and triumphs along the way.

Thanks to all those people who took part in my internet relationship survey. And a special thank you to all of my coaching clients who provided me with such wonderful insights into the world of human relationships.

I've had many great teachers since I set out on this path of self-growth. All of you have helped me in some way but I owe a special thank you to:

Joseph Riggio, who taught me how to step into the adventure of my own life and be truly myself.

Richard Bandler, the creator of NLP, whose genius inspired me and flows through my work.

Michael Neill, my coach, who helped me through the first stages of producing the outline for this book and shared his thoughts on relationships.

Jerry and Esther Hicks, whose Abraham tapes introduced me to some very simple and powerful philosophies.

I salute the authors of the many, many self-help books I've read, along with the facilitators of the many courses I've taken. You have all contributed to helping me reshape my life, rediscover who I am and develop my own skills.

A big thank you to the team at Element who recognized and nurtured my talent: Carole Tonkinson, who encouraged me to write the book I wanted to write; Jacq Burns, who took over Carole's mantle at a very crucial time and scythed her way through the first draft; Vicki Renner, for her enthusiastic promotion and encouragement; and finally Lizzie Hutchins, my patient angel of a copy editor, who contributed a clarity without which this book would have been a tad indigestible!

And finally, I'd like to thank all the men who have shared my personal relationship adventures over the years. You've been the greatest teachers of all.

INTRODUCTION

Our deepest fear is *not* that we are inadequate.

Our deepest fear is that we are powerful beyond measure.

It is our light, not our darkness, that most frightens us.

We ask ourselves: 'Who am I to be brilliant, gorgeous, talented, fabulous?'

Actually, who are you not to be?

You are a child of God.

Your playing small doesn't serve the world.

There is nothing enlightened about shrinking so that other people won't feel
  insecure around you.

We are all meant to shine, as children do.

We were born to make manifest the glory that is within us.

It is not in someone of us, it is in everyone.

And as we let our own light shine, we unconsciously give others permission to
  do the same.

As we are liberated from our fear, our presence automatically liberates others.

Marianne Williamson

WHERE WE ARE NOW: LOOKING ON THE OUTSIDE FOR WAYS TO MAKE OURSELVES HAPPY

'Teachers open the door, but you must enter by yourself.'

Chinese proverb

A 38-year-old woman came to me for coaching. I was alarmed when she pulled out a notebook and pen, saying, 'I've done the casual dating and the one-night stand thing and now I'm ready to do long-term relationships. I want to know all about how to do this dating/relating game.' As she sat there with her pen poised, waiting for me to pour out words of wisdom, I realized that what she wanted was a step-by-step set of foolproof rules, tips and techniques for having the perfect relationship. And that's not what I offer.

There are many books out there outlining techniques to 'guarantee' love, a perfect relationship or instant sex. They assume we all want the same thing. I think there's a difference between what we've been programmed to think we want and what we truly, deeply want.

As kids most of us learn that if we are in pain or unhappy, there's a magic make-it-better fairy such as a sweetie or a new toy. And the training continues throughout our lives. We are conditioned to look for solutions in the form of material things. 'If only I had more money, a larger house, a better job, my life would be wonderful ...' When we have a headache, we grab a pill to get rid of the pain. How often are we encouraged to find out what's causing the pain and taught how to prevent it by changing the way we act and react?

In the same way, when we feel emotional pain, we have been led to believe that a relationship or great sex will cure it. We hear people saying things like 'What she needs is a nice man to take care of her' or 'What he needs is a good woman behind him' or, even worse, 'Nothing a good seeing-to wouldn't sort out' – as if everything could be solved by a good shag! Sure, it's good to have great sex, but there are plenty of single people who are immensely happy and who don't have regular sex with another person! Good loving relationships and hot sex with other people are wonderful and can really enhance our lives, but they won't fix them. That's our job.

In fact, far from being a 'magic pill' that 'makes it all better', a relationship or sexual encounter entered into when we are feeling inadequate or unhappy often brings us even more pain.

Many of us have also been programmed to believe that marriage and a shared home and shared dreams are the ultimate aims of any intimate relationship, and if we don't reach these goals the relationship has failed. Yet almost half of all marriages are destined to end long before the grim reaper leaps in and tears us apart. And many people out there are living life in a very different way and still finding happiness – living in communes, sharing homes with same-sex friends, being married to straight people and having gay sex, living separately but in a committed relationship, having multiple partners, enjoying long-distance liaisons or living alone and maintaining a balance of positive relationships, both intimate and non-intimate. I suspect there are more flavours to relationships than vanilla, chocolate and strawberry!

Many women – and men too – are also programmed to believe that having children is the ultimate form of fulfilment. So why is it that many women with children still yearn for something more, whilst there are people who choose not to have children yet are very fulfilled?

Many of us have been programmed to believe that sex in a one-to-one long-term relationship is the only path to true sexual fulfilment. Why is it then that so many of us are indulging in sexual encounters outside our main loving relationship? What are we looking for?

The answer is that we've all been brainwashed into the one-track solution. But we are all unique and we all need to find our own route to happiness. And in order to do this we have to question some of the rules that we've been living by and create some new ones and say boo to those people who tell us 'You can't do that.' Wouldn't it be lovely to turn around and say, 'Sorry, I think I just did it – and I'm still alive and kicking!'

I don't guarantee that you can wave this book like a magic wand and make your life perfect. I do guarantee that when you are truly being yourself at your best, you will get everything you need and desire. And part of the 'Flirt Coach' philosophy is that once you are like that, your true flirtatious nature will bubble up naturally and enable you to use my communication tips and methods to get the most out of your life in your relationships, in the bedroom and even at work!

So how do you begin? First you have to be ready, then you have to make the decision to start and finally you have to continue to do what it takes to get what you want. Depending on how ready you are, reading this book may kick you into touch or may be the beginning of a lifelong journey of discovery and adventure.

If you can accept that no one and no relationship is perfect, and that working with the less-than-perfect is part of your life's education and very worthwhile, then you're well on the way to getting what you want.

WHAT KIND OF RELATIONSHIPS DO YOU ATTRACT?

What are your relationships like at the moment – alive and well or unhealthy and troubled?

- It might be that you're in a relationship that's just beginning and already you're trying to squash it into a box that wasn't designed for it.
- It might be that you and your partner are battling over almost everything because there are so many things that you've not discussed or resolved.
- Perhaps you are in a relationship that is disappointing because it isn't all that you expected, and you are blaming the other person.
- Maybe you are in a relationship and have drifted apart, yet still muddle through somehow, without much conflict but without much joy either.
- Perhaps you are in a relationship that you want to leave, but hey, it's a scary world out there and anyway 'it's better to be with someone than on your own'. But the longer you stay, the more resentment you feel towards the other person.
- Maybe you avoid getting too deep into relationships because you've learnt from bitter experience that if you expose yourself emotionally you're bound to be hurt.

If any of these are or have been true for you, this book has something for you.

WHAT DOES THIS BOOK OFFER?

Many books and magazines tell you that there's a chocolate-box perfect world
out there that you can magically enter when you learn how to give the perfect
blow job, or have multiple orgasms, or pass your exams in romantic behaviour –
but if they don't tell you how to have the attitude and beliefs that enable you to
do all of this, chances are you won't get the keys to that chocolate-box paradise.

What I'll be encouraging you to do is to look at the way you've related
intimately in the past and to learn from it. Even if your relationships have been
hell, there'll be something you can learn from them – if only not to go there
again! Then you can start to attract relationships that are right for you.

Stage 1: Your Story

The first step is to discover how you have been affected by primitive genetic
coding and years of programming and realize that you can (with some help)
become once again the natural, alluring, magnetic, wonderfully perfect person
you truly are.

Stage 2: Intuitive Communication

If you are going to find the right relationship for you, you have to be able first to
pick up and secondly to interpret your intuitive signals. I'll show you how to do
this and how to sharpen up your intuitive ability to sense signals from other
people too – invaluable in any interaction!

Step 3: Recognizing your Personal Conditioning Patterns

In this section I'm going to pull aside the curtains and turn the spotlight
on your personal beliefs about relationships and the patterns you repeat. As
you gain more awareness about how you currently relate, you'll be able to
understand what's stopping you from finding the love that's right for you.

Stage 4: Awakening your Natural Self

In this section you can work on dumping bits of old programming that don't
work, gaining a greater sense of who you really are, creating empowering beliefs
and unleashing your natural sexuality. You'll be getting ready for love.

Stage 5: Loving, Clarifying and Connecting

Now that you are more in tune with who you are and what you really want, you are ready to relate more naturally to other people. Love is just round the corner for you. In preparation for welcoming love into your life you're going to learn how to love yourself and others in a very special way, clarify your beliefs about major topics that dominate relationships and connect more fully with people.

Stage 6: Communicating, Creating and Building

In this part we're going to work on keeping and nurturing love. We take a look at how to use language and personal strategies to communicate more harmoniously with people and examine the attitudes and methods that, in my experience, are very effective in building and maintaining healthy relationships.

HOW TO GET THE MOST FROM THIS BOOK

This book is designed to enable you to find your own way to who you are and the love you want. Some of the 'explorations' and activities will help you to examine your character, your attitudes to other people and what you really want. They make it easier for you to override unwanted conditioning and retrain your brain to think in a more natural way. Some of them will make it easier for you to communicate more effectively with the people you love. All of them are based on a variety of tried and tested psychological techniques and the discipline of Neuro Linguistic Programming. I've used them on myself and my clients with great success.

You can choose to dip into this book, put it aside and come back to it or you may want to read it from cover to cover and do all the exercises whilst making notes on what's important to you. This book is all about learning to be natural and doing what you feel is right. So dump the guilt and do it your way.

The world is full of people telling us what to eat, listen to and even wear. And there's some great advice out there on how to live your life, but not all of it will be right for you. So please don't take everything I say as gospel. Instead, use the opportunity this book offers to work out what's right for you.

I know that you will take from this book whatever is most valuable to you, even if it is just one thing. But if that one thing sparks off a chain of events that leads to you uncovering some more magic in your life, then I've done my job.

Thank you for inviting me to join you at this stage in your life's journey. I trust that together we can open some doors, find out more about ourselves, have some fun, learn heaps and then part, moving on to the next adventure ...

CHAPTER 1

YOUR STORY

'You are the product of other people's habitual way of thinking.'
James A. Ray

Are you directing the movie of your life? Are you having lots of fun? Are you excited about what's round the corner or do you simply check the TV guides, slouch on the sofa and let it all pass you by as someone else or 'fate' makes your decisions for you?

It doesn't have to be like that. And if you're looking for love, you can't let someone else decide how or where you find it. You've got to get up off your backside and be the director and the star of your own adventure movie. You're going to have the final say in casting lovers and writing plots that will bring the proverbial happy ending. And you don't want it to look like a rehash of someone else's movie, do you?

YOUR HEROIC JOURNEY

Life has a very strong pattern and over the years people have been recording it in myths, fables and old wives' tales. These stories aren't fantasy, they're truths about how life really is. Joseph Campbell, the world's leading expert on mythology, discovered a common pattern running through myths from every culture he studied. He called this pattern 'the Hero's Journey'.

Many movies and books are based on the idea that when we answer the call to adventure, magical things happen and ordinary humans achieve extraordinary results. In the film *Star Wars*, Luke Skywalker leaves his farm for a life of adventure and challenge, as does Dorothy when she undertakes her epic adventure to the Land of Oz. Both of them were scared, yet they resisted their conditioning and listened to the voices they had inside them. Their inner guidance system told them to go for it – and look at how their lives changed for the better.

We've all got a Dorothy or a Luke inside us and most of us probably know someone who has let them out to play.

THE CALL TO ADVENTURE

'There is no security in following the call to adventure. But to refuse the call means stagnation and what you don't experience positively, you will experience negatively.'
Joseph Campbell

SUSAN'S STORY:
Moving On

Susan had been in a relationship for 12 years. It had had its ups and downs and they'd both made efforts to patch it up. She had a nagging feeling that she needed to be free but she would look around at her cosy home, her dog and her devoted partner and get scared and dismiss those thoughts. She resisted her call to adventure because she thought she wasn't ready and she was scared of change.

When, after 12 years of fidelity, Susan had a sexual fling, she realized that it was her body's way of kick-starting herself into action. She gave up her home, her dog and her partner. She was all alone and a little scared, but also very excited. And somewhere along the way, she read a few books and took some courses which led to her doing the work that was right for her. And then she found a new man who was exactly right for that stage of her adventure.

Like Susan, you may be thinking anything from 'I hate my life' to 'Something's not working here.' Maybe you're longing to move out of a relationship or change your job or deepen a relationship or even to ask someone out on a date. You may be feeling scared of making changes. We fear change more than anything else. But change is inevitable. And it can lead to great things ...

Hearing the Call

Are you completely content with the way your life is right now? Or are you aware of something that you've tried to ignore niggling at you from inside? It might be a thought that keeps running through your mind or something you want but don't think you can have.

- ♥ What's stopping you from going for it? What are you afraid of losing?
- ♥ What could you gain by answering this call to adventure?

THE ADVENTURE

When you get the call to adventure and acknowledge it, things tend to happen in a certain way.

1. A chance meeting or remark kicks in the belief that you can change and leads you to take action. It might be dumping someone from your life or quitting a job or throwing away that pack of cigarettes or buying a book like this.
2. When you take that first step, you'll probably experience a mixture of fear and excitement, but you'll have a feeling that you're on the right track.
3. It may not be plain sailing. Indeed, sometimes the odds are so stacked against you that you wonder if you'll make it through. But when you are really determined to stay the course, you'll be surprised at the support you receive from out of the blue, maybe in the form of people or opportunities that seem to appear at just the right time.
4. And when you least expect it you will meet that special someone or find the job that is just right for you.
5. But it doesn't stop there, because before you know it ... you hear the next call to adventure.

'Be a first-class version of yourself, not a second-class version of someone else.'
Judy Garland

Poor Judy Garland. Her talent was hauntingly unique and I suspect she desperately wanted to be herself, but she got caught up in the system that eventually destroyed her.

When you're being a first-class version of yourself, you're firing on all cylinders, balanced, open and raring to go. It's a magical combination of personal power, high self-worth, an open heart and a willingness to express yourself. It's very attractive ... but before you get there you may have to have a spring-cleaning session.

Most of my coaching clients and the people who attend my flirting classes have one common challenge. They aren't being their true selves and they can't see what they really want because they're surrounded by clutter. That clutter is their social and biological inheritance. We've all got it to some extent, but when we wise up we realize that we don't really need to keep Granny's old vase or Grandpa's worn shoes and that throwing them away might make room for our own stuff.

Let's take a peek at the social and biological conditioning that has the power to lead you off track and away from your natural self.

BASIC PRIMITIVE YOU

PROGRAMMED NEEDS

Unique as you are, you have many things in common with your fellow human beings:

- ♥ You are programmed with the desire to mate.
- ♥ You are programmed with the desire to be safe.
- ♥ You are programmed with the desire to find shelter.
- ♥ You are programmed with the desire to satisfy hunger.
- ♥ You are programmed with the desire to be social.

These programmes were built into our ancestors' DNA. They were essential for their survival. Today, though we live in a world far different from that of our ancestors, we share some of that original DNA and as a result we are still driven by our primitive programming. This can lead to problems.

The primary purpose in life for primitive man and woman was to mate and keep the species going. They needed a mechanism that would make them want to do that. Because it was so essential that this programme worked, it came with an inbuilt feelgood factor that would make people want sex with particular types of people for particular reasons.

'PRIMITIVE WOMAN SEEKS MAN TO ...'

Women produce a limited reproductive lifetime's worth of eggs, only one of which can be fertilized once a month. When supplies are limited, a product becomes more valuable. Each egg represents a great investment. So women are programmed to look for men who will be worthy of their investment.

Our female ancestor didn't have her own income or own her home and she didn't have nannies, crèches or maternity benefits. If she was going to bring a baby into the world she needed a man who could provide food, shelter and protection.

This primitive programme appears to have lingered on. Surveys over a period of 50 years revealed that women value a partner with good financial prospects twice as highly as men do. Social status is also valued because it is an indicator of power, which generally creates wealth. Women are programmed to look for intelligence for the same reason – intelligence is an indicator of the ability to generate wealth.

In a world where predators were rife, it's not surprising that women were also primed to seek out strong, healthy men. Strength was an indicator of a man's ability to protect his woman and child, and health was a sign that he'd stay alive long enough to do it!

Of course none of these resources were any good if the man didn't stick around to provide them. So women wanted a heavy dose of commitment as well.

Recent surveys have revealed that love, kindness and sincerity are still very important to women because they are indicators of a man's potential to commit.

If our female ancestor were to place an ad in the personal column of the *Stone Age Gazette*, it might read:

'Primitive woman seeks mate. Must be resourceful, strong and prepared to commit. In return promises she will look after the babies and provide regular sex.'

'PRIMITIVE MAN SEEKS WOMAN WHO ...'

If primitive man were going to place an ad in the lonely hearts column, his criteria would be very different. Men produce millions of sperm which are replenished at a rate of about 12 million per hour. All a man has to do to ensure the survival of the line is to get a woman pregnant. And physically speaking, he can impregnate as many women as he can get to consent to it. Man's primitive programming prompts him to spread his seed far and wide in the hope that at least a few children will survive and keep the line going. This seems to explain why even the most committed of men lust after other women.

Though men are not programmed to seek a single mate, they also realize that women are rather careful about whom they let into their parlour. This and the fact that offspring had a better chance of survival if both parents were around to look after them may explain why men have had to develop strategies that weren't inbuilt. In short, they had to accept women's terms and commit or go without. And the more desirable qualities a woman had, the more she could demand from a man. So willingness to commit meant that a man had a better shot at the highly desirable mates.

Early man was programmed to look for youth, because younger women are more fertile. Good health was also seen as a sign that a woman would be able to reproduce. Our primitive ancestors didn't have physical check ups, but they did have their own criteria for health, which over the years have become the criteria of physical beauty – full lips, good skin, lustrous hair, good muscle tone, a high level of energy and a youthful appearance.

Primitive men were also programmed to prefer shapely women with a waist-to-hip ratio within a certain range because that was also a sign of good reproductive ability. Recent surveys have proved that women whose waist-to-hip ratios don't fall within that desirable range do have more problems reproducing.

So men are more into looks than women because it's part of their primitive programming. In surveys carried out over a span of 50 years, men consistently rated attractiveness higher than women.

Primitive man also looked for signs of chastity and subsequently fidelity in a woman, because as a woman's eggs can hang around for almost three weeks waiting to be fertilized, he couldn't be sure whether he was the father of a child or not. And he wasn't programmed to provide for someone else's offspring!

Primitive man's ad might read something like this:

'Primitive man of substantial means, prepared to commit, seeks young, beautiful, shapely, faithful woman to provide lots of sex and healthy babies.'

It's not surprising then that men and women have such a hard time coming to terms with each other's needs and wants. According to Anne Moir and David Jessell, authors of *Brain Sex*, men and women's brains are actually wired differently and no matter how we try to assume sameness in the quest for equality, the fact is that we are not the same and we react differently to the world.

Each time women try to be more male in their approach and men try to take on a feminine aspect, they are going against their natural predispositions. When women can learn to value the maleness of men and men respect women for their feminine qualities and both can be happy with being who they are, we'll have a lot more harmony in the world of relationships.

UNIQUELY NATURAL YOU

'Until at least the twentieth century, we needed our social beliefs about marriage in order to survive ... but now we have a new revolutionary assignment and in order to carry it out, we must see that these notions are no longer relevant.'

Daphne Rose Kingma

We still carry the conditioning of our primitive ancestors, but we have evolved massively since those days round the campfire at no. 45 Cave Avenue. And as well as our primitive programming, many people believe we have an individual spirit or soul or essence programmed into our DNA. You might like to think of your DNA as your unique Deep Natural Assets.

When you were born you were utterly self-centred and completely alluring, and you had no reason to believe otherwise. You were totally confident, expected to get exactly what you needed and just being yourself was absolutely the best experience ever. And then you encountered the rest of the world and learned to be someone you are not.

DONALD'S STORY:

It's Not Always What It Appears to Be

Donald believed that his life would be sorted when he found a good relationship. He asked me to give him some tips on how to be more flirtatious.

During the session, Donald realized that before he even thought about serious relationship commitment, his first step was to develop the relationship with himself and start listening to his inner voice. I knew that when he discovered his special purpose in life and started being himself, he would begin to attract special relationships.

If you aren't attracting the relationships you want, it may be that you're not being truly who you are.

Are You Firing on All Cylinders?

This exploration is designed to help you get a sense of where you are now. And then you'll be ready to work on what you want.

- ❤ Even if you have what some might term 'a successful career', do you wake up every day and go to work with the sense of 'Yes, this is me'?
- ❤ Are you in a relationship for which you had high hopes and feel it's all going wrong?
- ❤ Have you had a series of relationships that you've considered failures because they didn't work out the way you planned?
- ❤ Have you not experienced a relationship at all and feel as if you are missing out?

If in general you feel that you are not relating in a way that is right for you, then read on ... It might explain a lot.

CONDITIONED YOU

'The hardest challenge is to be yourself in a world where everyone is trying to make you be somebody else.'

e. e. cummings

You were born with a blueprint for unique success, but somewhere along the line the world stepped in and systematic relentless social processing began. I bet you didn't wake up one day and say, 'These are the rules and beliefs and values by which I want to live my life.' No! You absorbed most of them unconsciously.

During your lifetime you've had a lot of things 'stirred into your pot'. Most of your ideas are those of your parents, church, friends, teachers and the media. And along with the good stuff, you've also been bombarded with loads of useless outdated rules and limiting beliefs. Let's look at where these have all come from.

YOUR PARENTS

As children, life is like sitting in a cinema watching a film being repeated over and over. The film is *Mum and Dad's Guide to Behaviour.* My friend Melanie has seen the film *Casablanca* so many times that she can act out every part almost perfectly! The roles our childhood guardians act out day after day become very familiar to us too. As we passively watch and listen, they are filling our heads with ideas and demonstrations of how life is and how it should be. Initially, these are our only experience of how life is.

Most adults think it's their duty to pass on their lessons in life so that their children don't make the same mistakes. Some of this can be immensely valuable and some of it is about as useful as a corkscrew on a desert island.

Our parents' first wish is to protect us from the perils of life, some of which may have happened to them personally. They tell us what they have concluded from their experience, for example:

'Money is the root of all happiness.'

'Success means having a good profession or trade or marrying someone who does.'

'Don't dream and you won't be disappointed.'

'People like us don't do that.'

'A woman can only be fulfilled when she's a mother.'

And they pass on their beliefs about relationships:

'Good girls get married and if you're not married at 40, you've failed.'

'Men are only after one thing.'

'Women want to get their hands on your wallet.'

'A lasting relationship is a good relationship. Relationships that end before death are failures.'

Parents also run guilt-trip patterns. You may have heard things like:

'We sacrificed everything for you.'

'We gave you a good education so that you could get a start in life, not run around playing music.'

'When are you going to make us happy and give us some grandchildren?'

'You owe it to us.'

But in their attempts to protect us from the challenges of life our parents sometimes forget that we are individuals. Also, they have had lots of programming themselves. So, often without knowing what they are doing, they pass on some of the not-so-useful stuff to us.

Check Out your Parental Programming

- ♥ What phrases or sayings do you remember your parents using to describe how life is?

- ♥ Does your family still have a hold over you? What do they do to maintain this hold?

- Do you hold any resentment or anger about your family? If so, have you tried to resolve it?
- Describe your parents' relationship. What did they do that you could see was or wasn't working?
- What family values and beliefs about relationships, love, marriage and sex did you inherit?
- Which of these go against your own personal feelings and which feel very comfortable for you?
- Does your family have hopes for you that aren't in tune with what you want?

LET GO OF BLAME

It's worth considering here that if you think you didn't get a good deal out of your childhood, the chances are that all those people who helped shape you didn't get much of a good deal either.

Parents and teachers and anyone who has a say in your guidance are simple human beings faced with the awesome responsibility for someone else's life. Most of them were just doing the best they could with no basic training and sometimes very limited resources. The chances are that they didn't have someone to remind them that it is possible to be loveable, adorable, desirable and respectable without resorting to game-playing or living a life you don't like. Letting go of blame makes more space in your brain for planning what you do want!

THE MEDIA

A journalist once asked me: 'Would you say that women are better flirts than men?' I said to her, 'Not really, but if you print that most people will probably believe it, won't they?'

It seems that we all have a need to find someone to tell us how to live our lives. Magazines are full of articles on how to give a great blow job or to seduce the person of your dreams. They tell us what women want and what men want, and we think that's how it is. But the media edit and manipulate and blur reality to create a false truth.

You've probably seen those stories in celebrity lifestyle magazines about stars in their perfect homes, cradling their perfect child and staring lovingly into each other's eyes. And then the next week we read that they've split up. This happens quite frequently. People expect celebrities to have extraordinarily wonderful lives and they are trapped into trying to live up to it. They are mostly insecure human beings, not gods, and their lives are not perfect. But we are led to think that they are. And that ours should be too.

Magazines don't just breed a desire for this 'perfect' lifestyle or relationship, sometimes they programme us into expecting the worst to happen.

The other day I read an article that said most relationships begin to falter at 18 months. The headline read: 'Is your relationship in the 18-month itch stage?' I can imagine people coming up to 18 months looking for evidence of the 18-month itch. And the more they look, the more they'll find.

Recently some statistics came out that indicated that after the age of 27 women's fertility declines. It was also stated that at the age of 40 the chance of getting pregnant was about 1 per cent. The magazine headline read: 'No hope for over-40 mums.' They're right – they're programming women over 40 to believe they can't get pregnant.

Whilst articles like this can be informative, they can also lead people to look for problems where there aren't any and to make very big mountains out of little molehills.

SELF-HELP BOOKS

Self-help books have done a wonderful job of awakening people to the possibilities of a better life. But they too are sometimes guilty of programming us into believing that what they advise is the only way. *The Rules*, for example, sold millions of copies because it promised a surefire route to marriage. And most women are programmed to believe marriage is the nirvana which releases us from all our woes.

Behind *The Rules* is the belief that the kind of marriage being promoted in the book is ideal. And the authors give examples of people who've followed the rules and got someone to commit. Of course they have, because they've played a game, pretending to be someone they are not!

LOVE SONGS

A love song can be a divine elixir that makes us feel wonderful or a toxic
story that poisons our system and sends us into deep depression. Unbeknown
to us, these songs are programming us with affirmations which develop into
beliefs about how life is. But it's frightening to think about what these
messages are:

> 'You're my world. You're everything to me.'
>
> 'You make me feel brand new.'
>
> 'You can make me whole again.'
>
> 'I'll never let you go.'
>
> 'If you go away, I'll die.'

These lines tell us that we can't be whole without someone to love us, that
when we lose love our life has no meaning and that other people are the only
ones who can make us happy.

Lines like 'You make me feel brand new' and 'Without you life has no
meaning or rhyme' are full of 'power-leak' language. They affirm to us that love
means surrendering control for our happiness to someone else.

We are also programmed to expect great highs and lows. We are told that
when we lose love it's natural to feel sadness, despair, regret, anger, bitterness,
self-deprecation and neediness. Lines like 'I just can't say goodbye' or 'I'll never
let you go' are programming us to believe that getting over a lost love is
impossible and so you start to develop the belief that it's OK to stay and wallow.
Perhaps it's no surprise that many love songs are written in despair by broken-
hearted people.

WE'RE COOKING TOO

We don't have much control over what gets coded into our programme in our
early years – we are sponges soaking up all the ideas, beliefs and ways of acting
and reacting that we are exposed to. We end up with a hotpot of ingredients and
other people's half-baked recipes for living. And we use this information as a
basis to develop our own recipes for dealing with life.

Your Story

RECIPES TO MEET OUR NEEDS

We all instinctively know when our basic needs aren't being met because we feel bad. And if you don't get regular doses of what you need, you begin to worry where the next portion is coming from. That fear is a painful emotion that triggers you to go in search of what you need.

TIM'S STORY:
Looking for Love

Tim was brought up in a home without much love. His parents went out to work and were often too tired for him when they got home. As a result he went seeking love. He needed constant reaffirmation that he was loved and was overly jealous and possessive and clingy.

Later you'll have an opportunity to discover what kind of needs you ended up with and how they were created. And then you'll learn how to meet these needs more naturally in ways that restore your inner power and make you very attractive.

HALF-BOILED BELIEFS

So we cook up our own pot of beliefs from the ingredients we get from other people and our own experience of what is going on around us and our reactions to it. There are a zillion situations that shape thoughts and beliefs. And depending on whether we are a passive acceptor or an auto-rebel, we either buy in or bow out. For example:

You may come from a family where people shout and scream at each other. So you could develop the belief that relationships involve a lot of shouting and screaming. Or you could resolve that you're never going to shout and scream when you are in a relationship.

You may grow up in a household where one parent blames and cries and the other parent just gives in. So you might develop the belief that crying and blaming make someone feel guilty enough to get them to do what you want. Or you might decide never to use such a painful and manipulative tactic.

You may come from a family where parent A's first concern in life is to keep parent B happy and where parent B acts in a very cold and detached manner towards parent A. So you could start to believe that being detached and cold gets you attention and devotion. Or you might decide that being detached and cold in order to get attention doesn't seem like much fun.

A lot of the time you make decisions based on what you've been used to. You will also learn rules for dealing with the information you receive. You may have been taught to question everything and make up your own mind or, more likely, you may have been taught to blindly accept the rules that have been laid down for you. But when you buy into someone else's system, chances are you'll end up with problems. What seemed to work for your parents, teachers and the rest may not have really worked all that well and it's probable that it won't be right for you.

MAKING UP THE RULES

Our beliefs lead to the development of rules for what to do and what not to do in certain situations. Sometimes we're very good at convincing ourselves that our rules are the best, especially if they appear to protect us. But sometimes the shields we think will protect us actually stop us from experiencing as much joy as we might.

ALAN'S STORY:
Love is Conditional

Alan wanted to be told that no matter what he did his parents loved him. Instead they only displayed pleasure when he got good academic results. They talked about how important it was to have lots of money and a good profession. Now Alan is a successful barrister, but he dreams of being a singer. He remembers the look of delight on his mother's face when he took her and his father to a fancy restaurant. He could hear her saying to herself, 'My son, the lawyer.'

Alan now has a belief that unless he showers a woman with presents, takes her on exotic holidays and generally spends money on her, he won't find love. And of course he gets girls, but he never feels loved, because the girls he attracts, just like his mother, are loving him for what he achieves and not for who he is.

A belief that might help Alan is:

There are people who will love you for yourself and not for what you've got.

NICK'S STORY:

Love Hurts

Nick fell in love with Lucy when he was 17. He opened his heart and wrote her sloppy letters. She rejected him. And his father told him: 'Women will break your heart if you let them.' Nick knew his father's words were true. He'd got proof that love hurts.

Nick decided that revealing his feelings created hurt and that if he closed his heart he wouldn't be vulnerable. He vowed never to fall in love with anyone again.

A belief that might help Nick is:

Not everyone will return my love and that's OK. Opening my heart allows someone to open their heart to me.

Many of us have felt emotional hurts from experiences past and present. If we haven't been loved enough, we need to find love. If we haven't been praised enough, we need to find praise. And if we haven't been touched enough, we seek the loving touch.

Maybe you have experienced something that felt bad and, like Nick, you have created rules for yourself to stop it happening again. And it's possible that following these rules doesn't make you feel as good as you'd like to.

Have you considered that what lies behind most painful emotions is fear?

Jealousy: When we are jealous of a loved one, aren't we afraid that we will lose the source of our love?

Envy: When we envy someone something they have, aren't we afraid that we'll never be able to have it?

Anger: When we get angry with someone, aren't we are afraid that they will be able to take away our power?

Lack: When we feel a lack of something, aren't we afraid that there will not be enough to go round?

Self-pity: When we feel self-pity, aren't we afraid that we can never be happy?

How it works:

1. You have a desire to meet your needs.
2. You create and follow dysfunctional rules and beliefs because you believe they will bring you what you need.
3. To fit into the system, you act out various roles and adopt certain forms of behaviour because you've seen them 'working' for other people.
4. You try to get what you need from your work or a relationship.
5. You learn to expect certain behaviour and attitudes from other people.
6. Things don't always work out and you experience painful emotions.
7. You blame other people for not meeting your needs.
8. You continue with this behaviour even if it doesn't get results, or
9. If you're lucky, you realize that it might be time to do something else because what you're doing isn't working!

YOUR BODY – AN EMOTIONAL FILING SYSTEM

Your beliefs and rules don't just affect your mind, emotions and behaviour – they are reflected in your body as well. Are you aware that your body stores all your beliefs, ideas and emotions in the very cells of its structure?

Scientist Candace Pert wrote a book about her research into the link between mind and body. She proved that our cellular structure changes constantly as our emotions change. And those structures are stored in the body.

When you feel painful emotions, you train your body into negative patterns and it shows on the outside.

MARTIN'S STORY:
Inside Out

Martin was 48 and just out of a long marriage. He had very little confidence in himself. When he walked into the room the first thing I noticed was his complete lack of sexual energy. He was bent over, chest caved in, and his head was drooping as he looked down. When he sat down, his hands folded like claws into his lap and he looked as if he was trying to make himself disappear.

I made him stand up, moved his shoulders back, shook him out and got him to breathe from his sacral energy centre, below his navel. I then encouraged him to speak from there. His voice went down a level or two and he had a big smile on his face. We did all this on national TV. Of course it wasn't an instant cure for Martin, but what it did give him was a glimpse of how changing the way he stands and moves can help to shift his feelings.

When you are creating negative thoughts, your body may undergo specific changes:

- Individual muscles may tighten and sometimes you 'forget' to release them for ages.
- Your face might be screwed up into all sorts of amazing contortions.
- Your fists may clench.
- Your spine may become more curved.
- Your stance may alter – you may twist round or put more pressure on one foot.
- Your knees might be locked one over another.
- One shoulder might be held higher than the other or both may be hunching.

It's kind of scary to realize that your body has been storing all that nasty stuff , creating an unattractive and unhealthy posture!

But there's some very good news too. As you change, the cellular structure of your body changes. So, with a positive attitude and some empowering beliefs, you can replace the negative stuff in your cells with positive stuff. And the more you do that, the healthier you become.

In the next chapter you'll learn more about how your unconscious mind is using your body to give you guidance on what's really right for you. When you begin to pay attention to the messages it's sending you, you can make significant changes.

CHAPTER 2

INTUITIVE COMMUNICATION

'You have to leave the city of your comfort and go into the wilderness of your intuition. What you'll discover will be wonderful. What you'll discover is yourself.'

Alan Alda

We all have the fantastic ability to know what's right for us and to sense important stuff about other people. Sometimes, though, we're just so full of hopes, worries and thoughts that we don't pick up on our intuitive messages.

SANDRA'S STORY:
A Real Womanizer?

Sandra was really keen on a fellow worker. He flirted heavily with her, which made her keener. He had a reputation as a womanizer and although she had 'niggles' about him, she dismissed them. Eight months after she started dating him she discovered he was still seeing his ex. Oops!

If Sandra had listened to her niggles and been more in touch with her intuitive feelings, she'd probably never have started a relationship with Mr Philanderer.

Fortunately, with a little practice you can become more aware of your feelings, the emotions behind those feelings, where they are coming from and what their message is.

You'll also learn how to recognize and interpret the signals other people are sending out. The more signals you pick up on, the easier it will be to create a full picture of what's going on and make decisions about how to react to the person sending these signals.

SENSING YOURSELF

'Intuitive feelings always guide you in a direction of growth and purposefulness. Listen to your body and it will tell you what you need to know.'
Wayne Dyer

GETTING IN TOUCH WITH YOUR FEELINGS

As you react to the world around you, you generate a cocktail of chemicals that whiz round your body and collect in various locations, causing different types of 'feelings'. The location of your feelings is directly linked to the types of emotions you are generating. Feelings linked to varying emotions occur in separate locations and feel very different. Being 'in touch with your feelings' is being aware of where they occur and why.

If you've ever had a physical ailment and described it to a doctor, you're already an expert in describing your feelings. If you were going to describe the physical sensations of your feelings you might use words like 'rhythmical', 'tingling', 'pulsating', 'dull' or 'pounding', 'fizzy' or 'light'. They may move rapidly or spread slowly. Each feeling is giving you a distinct message about a particular element of your emotional state. Being able to locate your feelings and catalogue them will help you to diagnose and balance your emotional well-being.

THE ANATOMY OF FEELINGS

You've probably had moments when you have sensed that what you are doing is really in tune with your natural self. And you've known instinctively when to say 'yes' and when to say 'no' to a request, a job or a person. The next exploration is designed to help you recognize your 'This is me' signals and your 'yes/no' signals. This will be particularly useful when you are interacting with other people or making decisions about what to do in your life.

Recognizing your Feelings

When trying to recognize their feelings, sometimes people report that they are all located in their head. This is quite common with analytical people. They will often describe them in a very calm way even when talking about highly charged stuff. This is because they are recalling the experience as an observer rather than reliving it as the subject. It's a bit like watching yourself in a movie on a faraway screen. You won't experience the feelings fully because you are disconnected from the events.

An easy way to get round this is to imagine stepping into the movie and reliving it as if it's happening all around you and you're seeing and hearing it with your own eyes and ears. This will help you 're-member' the feelings in your body rather than your head.

'This is Me'

- You've surely had those moments when you felt just wonderful, as if nothing could be more right. And you may have been thinking as you enjoyed the experience 'This is really me.'
- Take a moment or two to fully re-member one of these moments. If you're getting a visual or auditory effect, make sure you're seeing it through your own eyes and hearing it with your own ears. If you're watching yourself or listening to yourself, you're not experiencing it fully.
- Keeping the sense of 'This is me', scan your body and notice where you're getting the feelings.
- Place your hand on the location of your feelings and spend a moment focusing on them.
- Describe the feelings. Where do they start and where do they leave your body?
- Recall the moment again and when you get the feelings back, say something like: 'This is me and it feels amazing!'

Do this as often as you need to fully recognize your 'This is me' feelings.

Next time you're wondering whether what you are doing is right for you, check what you're feeling against your 'This is me' feelings. If you don't get the right feelings, it probably isn't right for you.

'Yes' and 'No'

I'm sure you can think of a time when you absolutely knew that something was right for you and you decided to go for it with a resounding 'Yes!'

- ♥ Go back to just before you made the decision and notice what you're seeing.
- ♥ If you are saying something to yourself, what is it?
- ♥ Where in your body are you getting the feelings and what are they like?
- ♥ Repeat this by recalling several different 'yes' decisions until you get a good idea of what you see, feel and hear. This is your 'yes signal'.
- ♥ Do exactly the same with a 'no' experience.

Next time you have to make a decision, check your signals and if you get a clear 'yes' or 'no', act on them. If the signal isn't clear, you may need to get more facts.

Remember, your intuition knows what's right for you.

THE ANATOMY OF ENERGY

'All truth passes through three stages. First, it is ridiculed. Second, it is violently opposed. Third, it is accepted as being self-evident.'
Arthur Schopenhauer

The ancient Eastern healing arts of yoga, chi kung and tai chi are based on the idea that the body is a mass of energy moving around in different ways and that harmonious movement and location of this energy is indicative of happiness and well-being. When you experience specific emotions, energy congregates in one or more of seven basic locations in your body.

Most Chinese medicine is based on the principles of these energy centres and their functions. The existence of energy centres along certain specific routes in the body (meridians) has always been accepted by half the world's population, but it has also recently been proven by scientific experiments. Scientists injected a reactive material into the body and filmed it with gamma ray cameras. These cameras picked up the fluid running along exactly the same lines as those described by the Eastern meridian charts.

THE ENERGY CENTRES

The seven major energy centres, or chakras, run in a line from the base of the spine to the top of the head. Awareness of the messages from your energy centres can help you diagnose which area of your life needs attention. The chart below and the questions accompanying it are designed to help you become more aware of your emotional make-up.

Energy Centre	Location	In Balance	Out of Balance
Root chakra	Base of the spine	You have a strong sense of belonging to a family or a social or work group. You will attract relationships with people who have solid roots and healthy family and social connections.	You may feel that you don't belong anywhere. You may find it difficult to join in family activities or socialize with your partner.

Energy Centre	Location	In Balance	Out of Balance
Sacral chakra	Two to three inches below the navel	You are creative, sexually open and in control of your life.	You don't feel in control of your life. You may be sexually repressed or lack creativity.
		You will attract relationships that foster your passion and sense of freedom.	You may be attracted to controlling or non-sexual relationships.
Solar plexus chakra	Solar plexus area	You like and value yourself and you are able to handle most of what life throws at you.	You may lack confidence, ambition or courage and feel unable to cope in a crisis.
		You don't need the approval of others to know you're OK.	You don't like personal criticism and you are afraid of rejection.
		You will attract relationships with people who have very high self-esteem.	You will look for a partner who boosts your confidence.

Energy Centre	Location	In Balance	Out of Balance
Heart chakra	Heart area	You find it easy to love, forgive, commit, accept and trust. You are also able to receive love openly. You will attract loving, compassionate and caring relationships.	You find it difficult to open out to love and/or to give love. In a relationship you may be critical and prone to commitment phobia.
Throat chakra	Throat area	You are able to speak your mind and communicate effectively. You will attract relationships where you are able to speak your mind and communicate effectively.	You may find it difficult to express yourself fully because you worry about what others think. You may resent your partner because you are constantly trying to keep them happy at your expense.

Energy Centre	Location	In Balance	Out of Balance
Third eye chakra	On the forehead, a little above and directly in between where the frown lines form	You make great decisions based on your gut feelings. You are very intuitive about other people. You attract relationships within which you are prepared to work on yourself and where you can co-create a relationship that works for you.	You don't know who you really are and find it difficult to know what's right for you. You may have a pattern of picking the wrong people and attracting very unsuitable relationships.
Crown chakra	Crown of the head	You have a sense of spirituality and connection to the world beyond. You will attract relationships with people who are willing to develop a spiritual as well as an emotional love.	You may be unethical or lack integrity. You are likely to believe that money or power is a route to happiness. You may look for relationships that are materialistically based.

If you want to test this out for yourself, make a resolution to be more aware of where you get feelings when you experience painful emotions and from time to time check with the table to see if they are in any way linked to the interpretations given.

To help you get to know your individual energy patterns better and work out where you might need some balance, try the following exploration.

Getting to Know your Energy Patterns

As you ask yourself the questions in each section, focus your mind on the area concerned. Where appropriate, it might help you to place your hand on the area as you think about the questions.

Root

Do you have a good solid circle of friends?

Do you belong to any groups or pursue any activities with a group of people?

Was your family home a haven, a boxing arena, a place of fear or fun or something in between?

Sacral

Are there areas of your life where you feel powerless? What are they?

How sexually free are you? How accepting are you of your own desires, quirks and needs as well as those of other people?

Do you feel you need to control others and if so, how do you do it?

Do you believe that you'll get what you need or are you always worrying about where the next penny is coming from?

Do you feel creative and if so, are you expressing your creativity fully?

Do you sometimes channel your creativity into negative things like gossip or put-down humour?

Solar Plexus

If you had to give yourself a rating for being a great and valuable person, what would you give yourself out of 10?

Do you need the approval of others or do you worry frequently about what people will say about you?

Do you have dreams of being and doing things, but haven't got off your backside to do anything about it?

Do you chide, criticize, dislike, hate or get upset with yourself?

Can you admit that you are wrong and be happy about it?

What positive beliefs do you have about yourself?

Heart

Are you comfortable with receiving love and easily able to show your love for someone else?

Do you sometimes use emotional blackmail to get what you want?

Are there still some hurts from past relationships that you need to heal?

Who loves you and who do you truly love?

Throat

Do you have a sense of what your unique purpose is in life and are you fulfilling it?

Do you know your own mind? Do you hold opinions and express them freely?

Are there times when you want to speak your mind but something stops you?

Third Eye

Do you sometimes get hunches but don't follow them up?

Do you often use your intuition or get gut feelings that you listen to?

Are you a good judge of people or are you just judgemental?

Crown

Are you able to learn from experience or do you tend to blame fate or other people for what happens in your life?

When you are in a relationship, are you able to evaluate what's happening from an objective point of view and accept that whatever happens, you are in some way responsible, even if someone betrays or victimizes you?

I find it useful to check in from time to time with each energy centre and ask myself how I'm doing. It only takes a few minutes to give yourself a quick check up. And if you get a sign that something is out of balance, you can get to work on rectifying it before it completely topples you over!

SENSING OTHERS

'We leak the truth from every pore.'
Sigmund Freud

Primitive humans were communicating with their bodies long before they learned to speak. As language developed we were trained to pay attention to words. But words only convey 7 per cent of the real meaning. If someone says, 'I'm fine' in a flat monotone voice whilst looking down, you can be pretty sure they don't really mean it. True meaning comes when words, voice characteristics and body language are in synch. Most of us can pick up on the obvious such as a wide grin or a big frown, but we often miss the tiny cues that are constantly leaking out.

Communicating with other people is like being in the middle of a busy traffic interchange. If you're not paying attention, you may not notice the signals changing. When you miss a red light you are putting yourself in danger and when you miss a green one you are losing out on an opportunity to move forward.

When you are able to pick up minute changes in people, you'll gain clues as to how to proceed. Becoming more aware might involve you doing more of something that seems to produce a positive effect. It may also require you to stop and ask clarifying questions. Either way, you'll deepen your ability to understand someone and that's the key to creating positive and fulfilling relationships.

THE ANATOMY OF SIGNALS

In my classes we always do interactive exercises in groups of three where one person takes the role of an observer. They are instructed to look for specific physical adjustments that occur when two people are communicating. The idea is not to interpret someone's movements according to a general map but to put what they do and say together to make an *individual* map of how that person expresses themselves and use it as a guide to ask more questions or change an approach or do more of what appears to be working. Here are a few things to look out for:

Posture

Is it upright or slumped? Is the person leaning forwards or backwards? Look for crossing and uncrossing of legs, keeping knees and legs tightly together or sitting with legs open. Notice how they use the space around them. Are they spreading out their arms? Are they folded in on themselves like a flower that is still in bud or are they open like a flower that's exposing all its petals?

Hand Movements

Are they clenching their fingers or playing with their hands? Are they gesturing to particular areas in the space around them or moving their hands away from or towards specific areas of their body? Are they folding their hands into their body or keeping them very still, covering their mouth when they talk? Look out for upward hand movement, no matter how slight, and ask if they're trying to say something.

Energy

Are they making slow deliberate movements or fluid ones, or moving rapidly or in a jerky way?

Skin

Look out for changes in skin colour. How and where does it change in relation to what they're talking about?

Breathing

When does their breathing slow down, speed up or become irregular? When are they holding their breath? Notice any sharp intake of breath or letting out of breath in a sigh.

Voice

Their voice tone, pitch, timbre, rhythm and/or rate of speech may alter. If they clear their throat or cough and they're not ill, when do they do it?

Facial Muscles

Their eyes may narrow or facial muscles twitch slightly. Sometimes people will put out their tongue, lick, purse or bite their lips. When are they doing this?

Eyes

Notice their eye movements. When do they move their eyes and where do they go? Sometimes people will look in a certain direction when thinking of certain types of experiences.

Nose

Pay attention to the nostrils. They may flare or twitch or narrow. Notice what they're saying (or not) as they do this.

A WORD ABOUT SMELL

As well as all the body language signals we pick up consciously, most of us are capable of unconsciously picking up smell signals. These are often very subtle. They are given off as the chemicals in the body mix together.

The olfactory nerve bypasses conscious thought and goes directly to the brain, which means that smells are the first signals we get. When people say things like 'I smell a rat' or 'That smells bad to me', that's their unconscious sense of smell working.

DEVELOPING YOUR SIXTH SENSE

'Life is like a ten-speed bike. Most of us have gears we never use.'
Charles Schultz

When you start watching and listening more closely to people, you may miss quite a lot because you may well be worrying about whether you're doing it right. But when you are able to put these unnecessary worries to the back of your mind and just relax and pay attention, you will become *unconsciously* aware of things. That's how intuition works. When all your senses are working efficiently it's as if you have a sixth sense.

So how can you be more intuitive about people?

THE SIX PILLARS OF PEOPLE SENSING

1. Feel open and positive towards the person you're communicating with.
2. Think of yourself as a detective on a mission to discover as many clues as possible.
3. Clear your mind of negative self-chatter and listen to the other person instead.
4. If you start to worry about noticing anything, just take a deep breath, let it out and relax.
5. Put aside interpretations and simply observe what's happening.
6. Ask questions to clarify the meaning of what you're picking up.

In the next chapter you're going to have the chance to delve into the types of relationships you create and how and why you interact with people the way you do. As you read, pay attention to your emotions and reactions to what you read. That way, you will find it easier to understand why you are the way you are and to become aware of what changes you want to make.

CHAPTER 3

RECOGNIZING YOUR PERSONAL CONDITIONING PATTERNS

'Remember that the best relationship is one in which your love for each other exceeds your need for each other.'

The Dalai Lama

Something to bear in mind as you read this chapter is that you may discover that you have behaved in ways that you do not like. Remember that your behaviour is not you. It's just a temporary demonstration of how you react to certain situations and conditioning, and it's all learned. What can be learned can also be unlearned, as you'll find out. So please resist the temptation to feel bad about yourself and instead choose to be happy that you now have the chance to do something different that will lead you to behave in a way that expresses your own unique and natural character and thus attract more harmonious relationships.

PATTERNS OF ATTRACTION

WHAT'S YOUR IDEAL?

'Releasing judgement of another is actually releasing judgement of yourself.'
Wayne Dyer

I bet you already have a good idea of the qualities you're looking for in an ideal mate or an ideal relationship. But have you ever considered that if *you're* looking for Mr or Ms Right and won't settle for anything less, Mr/Ms Right might also have similar criteria? How do you match up to your own criteria? Are you ideal enough to get that ideal person yet? And are you setting yourself goals that are impossible to reach?

In my experience, the more you begin to love, adore and value yourself, the more love-able, adore-able and value-able you become to everyone around you.

So, if you want someone who laughs a lot and is happy, *be* a person who laughs a lot and is happy. If you want someone to love you for exactly who you are, try loving *them* for exactly who they are, warts and all.

As you begin to explore your own patterns of relating, you will be encouraged to distinguish between what's naturally right for you and what's just an unwanted legacy from years of conditioning. Then you can begin to work on becoming more natural and more able to attract the love and relationships that are in tune with the real you.

YOUR BASIC ATTRACTION TEMPLATE

WHAT'S YOUR TYPE?

When I first met Susanna's new man I thought, 'I can see why she's attracted to him, but he's not my type.'

You'll probably have a type too, even if it's not immediately obvious. Your type is determined by the contents of your 'attraction template'. And your attraction template has been formed, and sometimes transformed, for a very long time.

The first thing I was attracted to in my boyfriend was his looks. I wanted him before I'd even spoken two words to him. That instant desire led me to engage with him and during our conversation I realize now that I was looking for other factors that matched my template. A good-looking guy is no good to me without a whole host of other stuff to go with it!

What had attracted me to men in the past had been a combination of looks, intelligence, attitude, energy and charisma. And I haven't had relationships with a series of clone-like men. I also realize that there were some very basic factors in my template and that over the years stuff had been added and removed as I'd grown and changed.

WHAT FLOATS YOUR BOAT?

So, what determines the basic contents of your attraction template?

There have been times as you're growing up when you've had good feelings and those feelings have been linked to someone. Something about that person has gone into building up your attraction template.

You may also have a template for things you don't like. This will be created in the same way. You've linked someone in the past to bad feelings and something has slipped into the template too.

It might be that a certain person had a particular body shape or way of gesturing or feature. These will build up your ideas of what is and isn't physically attractive, often for no logical reason at all. You may be attracted to someone because they remind you of a parent in some way or because they have similar features to you or because they look very different from you. There's no accounting for it, but it's very powerful indeed.

Some theorists believe that we are attracted to someone because their genes fit with ours. The idea is that if we have genes for weak lungs, then we may attract someone who has a gene for very strong lungs. These genes unconsciously cause us to emit various energy waves and they are picked up by our genetic match. That would make sense in the evolutionary scheme of things and it could be a strong explanation of 'love at first sight'. Perhaps it's not love but rather game set and gene match!

Our attraction template appears to have several categories and you will have your preferences in each of the categories.

Looks

Why are looks so important to many people? As you now know, many of the things that our ancestors recognized as signs of good reproductive ability have become what we define as 'beauty'. In addition, different cultures regard different physical features as attractive. In some countries it is very desirable for women to have curves and in others a more boyish look is attractive. And then each person has their own individual preferences.

The particular look that you go for will involve many things, including hair, body shape, gait, facial structure and height. You might go for eyes, mouth, bum, breasts, legs, hands ... and the rest.

It's possible that, like me, you've not always ended up with people who match your particular looks template. And that's because attraction has many other strands to it.

Voice

Many people are very attracted to the sound of someone's voice. So many women swoon over Sean Connery, for example, because his voice seems to surround whoever listens to him with waves of sensual and very sexy sound.

Energy

You will probably be attracted to a certain type of energy. You may like the fiery action-oriented fast-talking kind of person, or you may be drawn to a slow-talking and grounded type. They may have a way of moving that appeals to you.

Smell

Everyone emits various chemicals that make up their unique smell. These chemicals are known as pheromones. Though we can't consciously distinguish them, they affect us in a very powerful way. There's no rhyme or reason as to why you like the smell of some people and not of others.

Sexual Spark

Sometimes you can't help feeling a connection at a very deep sexual level. This is a genetically driven attraction to someone who seems to match your chemistry. Beware the sexual spark – it's hard to live without it, but it sometimes stops you from realizing that someone isn't really for you in the long term!

Behaviour

It's also possible that you meet someone who isn't your immediate physical type, but you are attracted to the kind of person they are.

If someone doesn't match your physical template, the immediate sexual spark might be lacking. But over time, personality and persistence can triumph and generate a much deeper and more lasting sexual spark. A friend dated a guy and then dumped him because he wasn't her type. I was surprised to find out a year later that they were getting married. She told me that he had been so persistent that he'd broken her physical template: 'He's a warm, caring and very sexy man and I love him to bits.'

'LOVE' AT FIRST SIGHT

You may know what it's like when you set eyes on someone and your heart beats faster, your breathing changes, your nostrils flare and the chances are you are ready to jump into bed with them right there and then! It's a very powerful feeling indeed and it makes people do the most extraordinary things. Some people call it 'love at first sight'. I think it's something very different.

In my view, this feeling is not instant love but instant lust. Instant lust makes us go weak at the knees and create a chemical mixture that shoots straight out of our pores at the other person. They smell, taste, feel and see it, and if it's mutual it appears to be love. But I reckon it's just a case of two templates wanting to tango together.

Lust is a highly efficient primitive device for kick-starting a potential pairing and it's great for fanning the flames of a good relationship, but it can also cloud our ability to make rational decisions.

It's the 21st century, not 1,000,000 BC and there's a lot more to creating a successful relationship than was originally required when our first DNA programme was installed. That worked superbly for our primitive ancestors whose only aim was to produce strong survival-oriented progeny. But we've come a long way since then.

So next time you look at someone across a room and feel those sensations, stop for a moment and remind yourself that you don't have to be led by lust, lovely and tempting though it is. You might want to take a deep breath and let it out slowly and then proceed with caution. But don't let that stop you having the time of your life!

UNRELIABLE TEMPLATES

As we grow and change, our templates take on new aspects, but sometimes they get stuck in a time warp and that can be dangerous, as a friend of mine discovered.

I was surprised when she confessed she was having doubts about her new relationship. They had loads in common, he was very spiritual and generous and she'd told me he was a great lover. But she confessed that she had niggles about the way he looked. 'He isn't my type,' she complained. Then I realized that she was still comparing him to the template she had in place when she met her first husband 30 years ago. He had been devastatingly good-looking. I reminded her that his good looks didn't stop him from being a control freak or dumping her and the kids and running off with a woman half his age.

YOUR NEED-MEETING ATTRACTION TEMPLATE
BASIC NEEDS

'To gain energy we tend to manipulate or force others to give us attention and thus energy. When we successfully dominate others in this way, we feel more powerful, but they are left weakened and often fight back. Competition for scarce human energy is the cause of all conflict between people.'

James Redfield

I was looking through a book about how to attract that 'perfect' person. The first rule was: 'Know what you want.' The paragraph started: 'You've got a lot of emotional needs and you want to find someone who's going to meet those needs.'

The question is, how needy are you? If you have a sense of being unloved, unwanted, undervalued, undesired and even underfed, you may be looking to a relationship to fill in the gaps big time. How healthy is this really?

PETE, MEGAN AND KRISTA'S STORIES:
Overriding Needs

Pete always felt sad that his father never played football with him. Now Pete's overriding need is: *'Spend lots of time with me.'* What happens when Pete's woman wants to go on holiday on her own?

Megan's father was very cold and distant and never cuddled her or told her he loved her. Now her adult demands are: *'Give me love and cuddles.'*

Krista's mother told her she was plain and would never be beautiful. Now Krista is always searching for a man who will *tell her she's beautiful.*

Krista, Megan and Pete's partners may find their demands a draining force on the relationship.

SYMBOLIC NEEDS

We weren't born with a taste for top restaurants, flash cars or red roses on Valentine's Day. As we've evolved socially we've come to associate these things with happiness, power and love. Many of us are also attracted to charm, romance, adoration or even disinterest. It's perfectly natural to enjoy all of these in moderation. The problems arise when we need more and more of them to convince us that we're happy.

Status

We may be looking for someone to provide for us. When they have status, we feel safe. We also feel some of their status might rub off on us and that boosts our self-esteem. 'My boyfriend drives a Ferrari.' 'My girlfriend is a film producer.'

What if the person loses the high-powered job or the Ferrari? If you are dependent on them, you may feel less powerful.

You are a person in your own right and can create all the status you need to feel good, because true worth comes not from outside, but from inside.

Charm and Flattery

Genuine charm and flattery can mean we are intimately interesting to someone. Conversely, a person may ooze charm or use flattery as a way of getting us to like them or break down our defences so that they can manipulate us.

Romance

Romantic gestures are associated with love. 'If he sends me flowers he must love me.' What if the person gives you flowers in order to make you think he's romantic? Do you need material demonstrations of love before you feel loved? How about if you loved yourself so much all you wanted from someone else was great interaction?

Adoration

Some people feel good if they are chased, even if they don't fancy the person doing the chasing. Do you need to be adored in order to feel good about yourself? If that's the case, are you giving them power over you? How adorable are you?

Disinterest

Some people enjoy the chase and when they've won the prize they lose interest. Holding back may attract someone who likes to conquer. But what then?

This exploration is designed to help you understand what you are currently driven to look for in a person with whom you want an intimate relationship. Notice which emotions come up as you do this.

- What physical looks are you attracted to – features, body shape, height, racial type?
- What material things attract you – possessions, job, status, social position?
- What personal characteristics attract you – romantic, charming, bossy, funny, needy, commanding, submissive, quiet, agreeable?
- What kind of energy are you attracted to – slow, quiet, fiery?
- What kind of sexual role do you enjoy playing? What turns you on?
- What did you need from your parents and didn't get?
- If you have ever become involved with someone because you thought they would meet a need, did they do so?
- Of the things you haven't got from relationships, which are you able to give freely?

WHAT MIGHT YOU ATTRACT AND WHAT MIGHT HAPPEN?

'Emotional needs can never be fully satisfied; they are an endlessly revolving kaleidoscope, ravenous, insatiable and huge. Moving beyond them is the only way to ensure they won't devour us whole.'

Daphne Rose Kingma

Remember that needy people are likely to attract other needy people even if their needs might not be the same. This can lead to some problems:

- If you attract someone who reflects your own behaviour, you may find yourself becoming very irritated by behaviour that you recognize in yourself.
- If you attract someone who refuses to co-operate with your needs, you may find yourself having to look inside to see whether you are doing something that doesn't work.
- If you attract someone who you think can 'fill your gaps', when you learn to become more self-sufficient you could resent them for trying to help you.

When you know how you operate, you can work out how to meet more of your needs by loving, valuing and respecting yourself more. Then you will attract very different kinds of people into your life with qualities that enhance yours.

PATTERNS OF RELATING

Most of us tend to do the same things over and over again. We run patterns and sometimes these patterns don't help us. If we can begin to understand what we do and the effect it has on us and on the people around us, we can work out what we need to change.

DATING PATTERNS

I suspect that you, like many others, have rules for dating. It might be useful for you to work out what these are and which ones don't seem to work. The following exploration is your chance to find out.

Your Dating Expectations

- When you are going on a date, do you have expectations?
- What dreams do you set up for dates and do they disappoint you?
- Are your expectations for yourself or for other people?

Sometimes we expect things from people that they can't give and then we are disappointed. It's worse if we don't have any uplifting standby thoughts to console ourselves with.

When you make a date with someone, what happens immediately afterwards?

- Are you excited, nervous?
- Do you zoom into the future and start to plan a life together or do you just plan a hot night together?
- What do you say to yourself? Is it encouraging or depressing?
- What kind of images do you make in your mind's eye?

What you say and visualize to yourself is conditioning you for how to behave on the date and will affect the vibes you'll send out. It's important to know what you are setting yourself up for.

Your Dating Beliefs

♥ What beliefs and rules do you have about who should do what?

♥ Do you believe, for example, that a man should always call a woman? Where do you draw the line? Is it OK for a woman to approach a man but not to ask him for a date?

♥ Have you ever thought of what would happen if you broke one or two of these rules?

♥ Whose rules are they anyway?

On the Date

♥ What really turns you off someone? Is it superficial stuff like how they dress or is it something more fundamental such as their religious or moral stance? Which might be a better standard of judgement?

♥ Do you start to size up your date from the very first moment?

♥ Are you ticking off a list or making judgements or are you just allowing yourself to find out more about them?

♥ Do you have rules that encourage you to pretend to be something you are not? Do you ever pretend that you're more sexually experienced than you really are or that you don't really want to sleep with someone because you are too 'nice' for that?

After the Date

♥ When the date is over, how do you react?

♥ Do you go back over it and wish you'd done something different or do you think of it as just another experience?

♥ Do you wait for the other person to contact you or are you prepared to make the next move?

Is the behaviour you indulge in before, during and after a date motivating and encouraging or does it make you feel worse or give you unrealistic expectations? Perfection is an elusive illusion.

Sometimes people set themselves up to fail because they unconsciously believe so strongly that they can't have something, they make it come true.

DAVID AND JACK'S STORIES:
The Perfect Woman

David wanted a perfect woman. He was an attractive man and was never short of great women to date. No matter what their endearing qualities, in the end David would always find some reason why they weren't quite good enough. Some of his reasons were so ridiculous, it was obvious to me that he'd never find Ms Perfect. He's been single for eight years and although he told me he desperately wants to settle down and have a relationship, I suspect that he's deliberately blocking himself. David will have to do some serious soul-searching and growth if he is to make progress.

Jack told me all about his perfect woman. He also told me that he believed he was defective because he was short. He'd made up his mind that he'd never find the perfect woman because if she was so perfect, why would she fancy a shortie like him? Jack's right – he will never find her because he's set himself up not to!

What if we went on dates simply expecting to have a good time and to enjoy finding out something about another person? And then, if that person was nice, we could ask what's next ...

ROLES WE PLAY

Whether on a first date or in a long-term relationship, most of us have found ourselves playing certain roles because that's how we think people want us to be. We adopt learned behaviour because we think that's the only way our needs will be met. Relationships are often the stage for some of the world's greatest actors.

HOW WE LEARN TO PLAY ROLES

Learning how to play roles is part of our conditioning. From childhood onwards, we've seen people acting in ways that seem to get them what they want. So we try them out ourselves.

Some of the roles we learn to act out are positive and helpful. But some of them are not. My aim is to help you recognize the roles that appear helpful but in reality are giving us as much success as a farmer might get trying to plough his field with a table fork.

If we were able to stick around to see the results of being someone we're not, we might think twice about our behaviour. For example, if we see someone throwing a tantrum to get what they want and we see another person giving in, we will register that a tantrum equals getting what you want. What we don't register are the bad feelings that both the tantrum-thrower and the person on the receiving end are getting. And somewhere along the line it's possible that someone might stop giving in and walk away because it's all too painful ...

TYPICAL ROLES

We are very fond of typing ourselves. That's why we love astrology and personality asessment tools (according to the Myers Briggs personality assessment). These aspects are only a small aspect of what makes up our persona and they're very useful within limits. But if we live by our labels, we're closing down other possibilities.

Here is a summary of many of the common roles that people play in relationships. As you read, please resist the temptation to pigeonhole yourself. Instead, realize that most people playact in some way and that you can choose roles that help you or roles that hinder you. Use the awareness to help yourself move on rather than to beat yourself up! Ask yourself: 'Am I doing something like this and if so, how is it hindering or helping me and what could I be doing instead?'

The Saboteur

Sam rarely expects that anything will go right for him. A friend once set him up with the perfect business opportunity. Sam got sick the night before the meeting and couldn't make it and then found all kinds of reasons why it would never have worked anyway. On a first date with a girl he quite liked, he turned up an hour late. He was also late on the second date. When she didn't return his calls, he said to himself, 'I don't blame her, no one can cope with my lateness.'

The People Pleaser

Paula wanted to be friends with the in-crowd at school. She would go along with whatever they said in order to be liked. Even when she didn't agree, she would nod her head because she was convinced that if she went against them in any way, they wouldn't want to be friends with her. As a teenager and in her early twenties, Paula slept with many men because she thought that was a way of making them like her.

The Attention Seeker

Veronica's father left her mother when Veronica was 15. Her mother always complained that if he hadn't left, they'd all be happy. Now Veronica looks for men who will be there for her. Whenever she feels that her lover is moving away from her, she begins to develop serious problems that require all his attention. She does everything she can to make him feel guilty and blames her problems on his lack of attention.

Peter Pan

Eddie is 47 but lives life like a child, carefree, without a thought for tomorrow. In terms of relationships he's a committed non-committer. He has been through a series of relationships that mostly end when the woman gets fed up trying to get him to settle into a 'grown-up relationship'. Eddie is also very concerned with youthful looks. He remarks that people 'look young for their age' and says things like 'Thank goodness I've still got all my hair.'

The Saviour

Julie always attracts men who have prospects but are 'flawed'. She wants to help them uncover their potential. She feels good when she can help a man change for the better, but her problems start when they no longer need her to make them feel good.

The Placator

Jim is very placid and hates confrontation and arguments. He believes his role in life is to make a woman happy. He will go out of his way to do everything to protect his lover from stress and pain, often denying his own needs in order to please her. But if she isn't content, Jim feels a failure.

The Provider

Tony was brought up to believe that a man's role was to climb the corporate ladder, provide for his wife and children and be a king in his own castle. Now he has to be in charge and responsible for his dependants in order to feel good. What will happen to him if he loses his job and is no longer able to provide?

Daddy's Little Princess

Beverley was Daddy's little princess. Her father had risen from poverty to great riches. His credit card catered for her whims for designer clothes, parties and holidays. Her mother described Beverley as 'very high maintenance'. Now Beverley only feels loved when she is being adored and all her demands are met. What will happen if she is with someone who loses his job or goes bankrupt?

Mummy's Bully Boy

Frank had a very controlling mother. She would criticize everything he said and attempt to rule his life. Frank married a woman who was very meek and mild. He couldn't control his mother, but he can control his wife. He is jealous, possessive and demanding. Because when he doesn't have anyone to control, he feels out of control.

The Perfectionist

Sally is a perfectionist. She worries about what people will say and never discusses her problems with her friends. She works hard to present a picture of the perfect marriage, but this puts her under severe stress and her sense of self-worth is always dependent on other people's approval.

The Attraction Addict

Dean is a very charming, attractive man. He is very quick to put a woman on a pedestal. Women who encounter him think they've found the answer to their dreams. Most of them are devastated when he dumps them because they aren't goddesses but normal human beings with flaws. Even if one day Dean does commit to someone, it's likely he'll be a philanderer, having to find new women all the time to make him feel good.

This is just a small sample of the roles people play in order to draw others into fulfilling their needs. I'm sure that as you read, some thoughts came to mind about the kind of things you do. Now for some more self-assessment.

What Roles Do You Play?

The purpose of this exploration is to be aware of what you do so that you can use the techniques outlined in the next chapter to work out better ways of meeting your needs.

- ❤ Which, if any, of the above roles do you relate to most (it may be more than one)?
- ❤ What do you usually get when you act like this?
- ❤ What don't you like about being like this?
- ❤ What do you want instead?

MODERATING ROLES

Remember each role that you play has two sides to it. It's fine to exhibit moderate doses of rescuing, pleasing, controlling and so on, as long as we're not sacrificing ourselves in the process. But acting out roles to extremes can damage our relationships with others. And sometimes our do-good instincts can become do-harm actions.

If we are a rescuing sort of person, for example, then rescuing someone, especially someone we love, may appear to be a naturally helpful thing to do.

Yet we need to consider whether what we are doing is really in their best interests, and our own.

Coming to the Rescue ...?

Patricia was very jealous and hated Jack looking at other women. Jack is a natural rescuer and his first instinct was to keep his eyes to himself in order to save her from her jealousy.

Then he realized that if he did this he wouldn't be helping Patricia to overcome her jealousy. He decided that instead of rescuing her, he would continue to do what came naturally whilst reassuring her that he loved and cared for her.

Patricia finally worked through her jealousy and Jack didn't have to sublimate his natural tendencies in order to keep her happy. Their relationship is much better as a result.

So, next time you reach out to rescue, organize or please someone, it might be worth asking: 'Is this truly going to help them or me?' and 'What else could I do to help them help themselves?'

RELATIONSHIP RECIPES

People will continue to do what they do until they realize it isn't working and then they just might do something else.

Many of us co-create relationships with a certain kind of person because we think they can make us happy and meet our needs. But it's more likely that we are unconsciously creating those relationships because we have a lesson to learn that will help us grow out of that neediness.

I believe that sometimes relationships are painful because we're looking for each one to be the magic formula to happiness and when it isn't, we're disappointed. But maybe these people were exactly what we needed to point out to us in some way that the answers lie not with them but inside ourselves.

Each of us is unique, but when you look at how people relate it's amazing how many common patterns emerge. I'm going to give you a peek into various patterns that have been noticed by psychiatrists, therapists and all those experts who spend time analysing us.

As you read I invite you to pay attention to your feelings and notice where and when they occur. They will let you know if something rings true for you. And later you'll have a chance to examine your own relationship patterns and make some choices about your future.

REFLECTIONS AND DEFLECTIONS OF MUM AND DAD

Some of us are attracted to people like our parents. We get used to our parents and if someone displays a similar characteristic to them, it will be familiar, so we will feel comfortable and will add it to our attraction template.

Sometimes we are drawn to positive traits. A good relationship with a loving father, for example, may lead you to a similarly loving man. Sometimes we are attracted to problematic traits. A relationship with a dominant parent might lead us to a relationship with a dominant person or we may become dominant ourselves. Sometimes we deliberately avoid people who display the characteristics of certain parents. If a man had a controlling mother, he may look for a woman who is very compliant. Many of our relating patterns are reflections or deflections of aspects of parental behaviour.

JOHN AND SUSAN'S STORIES:
Emotional Distance

John was attracted initially to the beauty, social skill and charm of his wife because his mother was a woman of great social standing. She was also quite cold! As time went on John began to see his wife as shallow and manipulative.

Susan was attracted to a very intelligent but emotionally distant man who was also good fun, just like her dad. She learned to enjoy the intelligent discussions, let him do emotions his way and feel good about herself anyway.

Some people are attracted to people who will play a corresponding parent/child role with them.

JOHN AND MARIA'S STORY:
Husband and Mother

John's mother took care of his every need. He married Maria because she too was kind and nurturing and he wanted to be taken care of. Now Maria has become not only a mother to her children but also to John. He often refers to her as 'Mother'.

What happens if Maria decides she wants to spread her wings and take up some activity that leaves less time for John? How might he feel? How might *she* feel if he pressurizes her to give less time to her activity and more to him?

What parental patterns do you have? Check it out with the following exploration.

What Parent Patterns Are You Following?

- ❤ What qualities did you like/dislike about your parents?
- ❤ Are you like either of your parents?
- ❤ Have you been attracted to anyone who appears to have a quality or qualities similar to those a parent had?
- ❤ What have you learned from this about the patterns you follow and how useful they are?
- ❤ What's it like when you are being truly yourself?

OVER AGAIN OR NEVER AGAIN?

Sometimes we get into these family patterns and even if they aren't wildly fulfilling we cling to them because they are familiar and therefore safe.

GRACE'S STORY:
Being Responsible

Grace was the eldest of four children. Her mother was in bad health and Grace often had to take on the role of mother to her brothers and sisters. She had little time for friends or fun. When she met Tom, she didn't realize it but she was attracted to him because he looked as though he needed help. He was disorganized and had a hard time keeping a job. As a result Grace once again found herself with little time for friends or fun.

Sometimes we seek a relationship with someone who is just like a parent in the vague hopes that we can change them.

ANNA'S STORY:
Changing Him

Anna's father was very critical and cold towards her. She married Dennis, who was very similar, and spent her entire marriage trying to turn him into the man she wished her father could have been. When Dennis refused to change, Anna's anger and his resentment at 'being changed' eventually broke up the marriage.

Sometimes our memories of parental behaviour or a particular relationship pattern are so painful that we are motivated to avoid it at all costs and often go to the other extreme.

JIM'S STORY:
'Flirts are Trouble'

Jim used to be attracted to outgoing charismatic women. His last two girlfriends had been very flirtatious and had both dumped him for someone else. After that, whenever he met a flirtatious charismatic woman he backed off, despite feeling very attracted. His next girlfriend was very quiet. Jim didn't feel a great spark with her, but he felt safe. Yet by avoiding women who had even the smallest hint of a flirtatious nature, Jim cut himself off from a lot of fun.

Are you missing out on something because you've been put off? Fear may keep you safe, but it closes a lot of doors.

'FILL MY GAPS'

How often have you heard that phrase 'my other half'? Julie told me she likes to think of her husband as her 'other 100 per cent' instead. But sometimes we look for someone to make up for our own weaknesses in the hope that their qualities will rub off on us or will fill a gap we can't fill ourselves. So a person who finds difficulty expressing themselves may select a partner who is very talkative. Someone who is emotionally cold might seek an open-hearted partner.

Someone who's not very bright might be attracted to someone who's very intelligent. Someone who wants to rebel but daren't might be drawn to a revolutionary.

DES'S STORY:
Being Sociable

Des was shy and quiet. He found it very hard to socialize, but he found himself attracted to very social, charismatic women. When they went to parties, Des was always the one who wanted to leave first. Many of his women felt hampered by Des's lack of sociability and his pressure to stop doing what they were enjoying. What was supposed to fill in for Des's weakness became a source of discord.

When you are attracted to a particular person because they have qualities you want, the relationship can work wonderfully well provided you are prepared to see the other person as someone to learn from, not someone to do what you feel you can't.

So if the would-be rebel is encouraged to take more risks by their rebellious mate, fantastic, and if someone who is emotionally cold learns to open their heart, wouldn't that be a positive result?

'MIRROR, MIRROR ...'
Sometimes we're attracted to people who unconsciously remind us of ourselves. This can be great and it can also become very competitive or confrontational.

KATE'S STORY:
'He's Just Like Me'

Kate's lover Tom was a controlling and stubborn man. He was also charismatic and great fun, just like Kate. Problem was, they both tried to control each other and refused to back down. Soon what attracted Kate to Tom was also what drove her away. But she's still excited whenever she meets a man who's 'just like me'.

Most celebrities are attention seekers and many have sought this lifestyle because the fame and adoration provide a great disguise for their insecurity. When two insecure attention seekers are attracted to each other and are getting equal attention, that's great. When one gets more attention, the other may feel hurt and jealous. That can cause major problems. But when both partners are sufficiently secure, each can bask in the attention the other is receiving.

'WOUNDED MAN SEEKS HURT WOMAN ...'

Don't for a moment think that I'm suggesting you are the only one with all the unresolved 'stuff'. There are so many 'wounded' people out there that the chances are that until you begin to cast off the stuff and let your true self out, you're going to attract someone who also has 'stuff'. You may not recognize it, and it may be very different from yours, but it will be there. So there you are, two imperfect people looking for perfection, and in some way you are meant to help each other ... Whatever next?

When considering a relationship, it may be useful to ask just how much you are looking to another person to help you repair your losses or fill your bucket.

And it would be equally useful to check out what you are doing to fill *their* bucket and how that works for *you*.

And what would it be like if you were filling up your own bucket?

And each time someone shows up in your adventure, you'll be making the relationship journey.

THE RELATIONSHIP JOURNEY

Being in an intimate relationship is like going on a journey of discovery with a travelling companion. You can enjoy the ride or maybe for some reason (sometimes for a very good reason) one of you just has to get off and go, leaving the other person behind. Some people don't get beyond the first station and others go right to the end of the line together.

Here's how many aspiring 'happily ever after truly romantic relationships' progress:

1. Attraction

You see someone across a room. You are deeply attracted. The sparks fly ...

2. Infatuation

For the first few months, or years, your hormones keep you high. You are besotted with each other and you believe you've found that perfect partner. Your rose-coloured glasses filter only the wonderful things into your vision.

3. The first glitch

Sooner or later you have your first row or serious disagreement. All is not perfect. The rose-coloured glasses lose their tint as you each reveal a little more of your pitiful humanity. Generally you patch things up and move on, a little wiser and a little less infatuated.

4. The hidden agenda

If you are both needy, then in time more and more of your hidden needs and patterns begin to surface. Your partner may not be the cure-all for what ails you. You may begin to realize you're on the wrong life path. Both of you may be struggling with your demons and sometimes things get so bad that you go off the rails altogether and you blame the other person for not making you happy. Many relationships end somewhere during this period.

5. Reaching rock bottom

If you stick it out, you might reach rock bottom, perhaps sparked off by an affair or a job loss or the discovery that you can't have children or one of you experiencing a powerful life change that alters the status quo. Sometimes it's too much and you quit.

6. Awakening and renewal

And sometimes hitting rock bottom is your relationship wake-up call. You may decide that what you have is too precious to lose and with time, patience, effort and love, you work through your challenges and emerge refreshed and renewed. Generally, when a relationship passes through this stage, it can survive anything life throws at it. So next time you hear a happy couple say 'We've had our ups and downs', know that they've worked really hard to preserve that relationship.

Some people associate longevity with success, but is making it last more important than enjoying it? Sometimes those journeys are one long compromise and at the end you might look back and think, 'Why didn't I get off at that station when I had the chance?'

Looking Back on your Journeys

It may be useful to think about your past relationships in the context of this journey.

- ❤ Consider what stages you reached.
- ❤ What made you quit at a particular stage?
- ❤ How could this prepare you for the next journey?
- ❤ What might you want to do differently?

STORMS PASS AND WE EMERGE

'Happiness is when what you think, what you say and what you do are in harmony.'
Mahatma Gandhi

Relationships are seas in the ocean of life. As we sail, we encounter storms, gentle waves and calm waters. After each storm there is always calm, though we know that life is never plain sailing. With each new journey we face challenges, but the more we sail, the greater our skills become. And some of us are destined to wander forever while others may decide to cast anchor in a suitable port.

So far we've been programmed with ideas and beliefs, played a few roles, followed some interesting patterns, had some relationships and experienced some empowering and some painful emotions. By now you may be thinking, 'Perhaps it's time to set another course.'

Perhaps it's time to awaken your natural self ...

CHAPTER 4

AWAKENING YOUR NATURAL SELF

'A person's judgement of self influences the kinds of friends he chooses, how he gets along with others, the kind of person he marries. It affects his creativity, integrity, stability and even whether he will be a leader or a follower. Self-esteem is the mainspring that slates each of us for success or failure as a human being.'

Dorothy Corkille

Low self-esteem is like a virus that sneaks in and slowly chips away at your mental immune system. When that happens it's very difficult to attract the love that's right for you and to maintain healthy relationships.

On the other hand, when your mental immune system is in good shape:

- ❤ You like yourself, you enjoy the work you do, have a good group of friends and generally love life.
- ❤ Your self-image is that of a sexy, powerful and confident person.
- ❤ You find it easy to speak your mind and be natural.
- ❤ You know what you want and what's right for you.
- ❤ And you attract happy, fulfilling relationships that work for you.

If you want more of this and less of the 'I'm no good' and 'Poor me', then the various processes in this chapter might be just what the doctor ordered. They are designed to help you value yourself more highly, enhance your confidence and give a wake-up call to your dormant natural self.

VALUING YOURSELF

There is no comparison when it comes to people. You are a winner in your class.

HOW WONDERFUL, AWESOME AND MAGNIFICENT ARE YOU?

Earlier, I encouraged you to access your 'This is me' moments *(see page 21)*, the moments when you are being wonderful, awesome and magnificent. When you are like that, anything is possible and people are drawn to you like magpies are to gold.

Sadly, most Brits and Northern Europeans are taught to value modesty and practise self-deprecation, whilst self-praise is dismissed as a form of boasting. I don't think it's boastful to recognize your talents and qualities and to be OK about talking about them. You're expected to do this in job interviews, so what's different about doing it in other situations? If *you* don't extol your special magic, why should anyone else?

In my classes I get people to make a list of what they love about themselves. Quite a few of them sit staring into space for a long time with an empty piece of paper in front of them. Some of them get quite upset when they realize they can't think of anything to write. There's plenty for them to write, but they just haven't been trained to focus on it.

Whilst we are amateurs at the art of self-love, most of us are very skilled and professional self-effacers. But I honestly believe that you are naturally magnificent, wonderful, splendid, awesome, or whatever word you want to use. And you are no less awesome or magnificent than the next person.

EXPERIENCING YOUR MAGNIFICENCE

Have you noticed how many personal ads have lines like 'My friends say I'm good-looking'? What's wrong with simply saying 'I'm good-looking'?

If I asked you to write a paragraph praising the virtues of your best friend or your favourite restaurant or piece of music, I bet you'd find it easy. How easy would you find it to do the same about yourself?

DAWN'S STORY:
'I'm a Great Dancer'

When I asked Dawn to tell me what she liked about herself, she put out her fingers and struck each one as she rattled off very quickly: 'I'm kind and caring. I'm good at my job and I'm adventurous and I'm a great dancer.' She sounded about as enthusiastic as she might do when talking about a cardboard box.

Dawn wasn't experiencing herself in the first person. She was like an observer standing outside her body. When we do this, we don't sense our feelings properly and our description becomes like a tiny out-of-focus black-and-white photograph. The reason we do this is because it feels safer. If we begin to feel and see ourselves in Technicolor glory and booming sound, it gets scary. 'You're full of yourself' conditioning pops up and we try to get some distance from it.

I wanted Dawn to really feel what it was like to be herself at her best. I asked her to stand up, close her eyes and think about dancing. I knew that this would make her re-experience the moment before she could describe it.

Before she began to speak at all, she began to move. She raised her arms and stretched them out and began to twist her wrists and hands. She lifted her head, looked ahead and took in a deep breath. As she started to move, her tongue came out and licked her lips. And then she began to swivel her hips.

She said, 'When I dance it's as if I come alive. Dancing makes me feel so empowered, so ...' and she stopped talking. She looked very sexy. She was giving out a powerful vibe. She was showing me her best self and loving it.

What's Great about You?

Now it's your turn to experience how wonderful you are.

If you haven't yet read the quote from Marianne Williamson at the beginning of this book, please go back and do so before you do this exploration *(see page vii).*

Awakening Your Natural Self

If there's a piece of music that makes you feel great, put it on or hum it to yourself or play it in your head.

Stand in front of the mirror and smile at yourself. Take a few moments to look your body up and down, noticing only what you like.

Spend some time thinking about your 'This is me' moments and make sure you are in your body and not observing yourself from outside like Dawn was. Then write down the answers to the following questions:

- What's great about you?
- What are you good at?
- What are you proud about?
- What do your friends like about you?
- What physical attributes are you most proud of?
- What makes you loveable?
- What special gifts would you bring to a relationship?

If you get any negative thoughts coming up, flip them over or move on to something else. If you keep thinking, 'I've got a big nose,' find a part of your body you do like!

Write in the present tense. Here's a sample of how it might start:

'What's great about me is my ability to see the good in everyone. I've got a cute bum, I'm a wizard in the kitchen and my friends love the way I am able to listen to their troubles without giving advice ...'

And if you're saying to yourself, 'I wish I were more ... but I'm not,' write it in this way:

'I am allowing myself to be more ...'

When you finish, put your hand on your heart and read the whole piece to yourself.

Imagine that you are wrapping the paper tightly round an arrow and firing it from your heart towards everyone around you.

You can fire your imaginary arrows in every social situation, whether on the bus or at a party. Next time you encounter someone you want to get closer to, imagine firing your arrows at them. If you are in a relationship, do this with your lover on a regular basis. The more you do this, the more they'll feel something coming from you. They won't know what it is, but they'll like it. Because, like you, they're intuitive souls and they pick up on good vibes.

Find your Special Word

Alain thought, like many of us, that having a great relationship would fix his life. I, on the other hand, thought that if Alain could have a fantastic relationship with himself, his life would automatically fix itself. I did the above process with him and watched him shift. He seemed to shed years and began to glow.

It's important when doing a process like this that you have some kind of reminder that will bring back the sensations. Often one word is enough.

I asked Alain what was the first word that came to mind when he felt like this. His word was 'happy'. He kept repeating it: 'I'm just happy.'

When you think about what's great about yourself and re-read what you've written, what word or phrase comes up for you? Go with whatever comes first. It's probably going to be something very simple like 'happy' or 'content' or 'smiley'.

Repeat this word to yourself often; it will trigger off the good feelings in you. Use it whenever you can in conversation or writing. Put it on a computer screen saver, paint a picture of it. Do whatever it takes to remind yourself. And soon it'll be part of you – and then what?

When I've done this process with clients, I ask them, 'And like this, what's possible for you?'

They all answer the same thing: 'Anything.'

And it's true. Like this, anything is possible ... provided it's in tune with who you truly are.

FORTIFYING YOUR PERSONAL POWER

THE POWER OF THOUGHT

'Your thoughts are all seeds that you plant. What you think and talk about expands into action.'

Wayne Dyer

How you think about yourself has an immense effect on how you react to situations and how other people react to you. Each thought we have changes the chemical compositions in our body and the body is constantly emitting a complex web of energy signals – heat, cold, smells, movement and sound.

Every day you will think millions of thoughts and unless you've had a really positive upbringing or done a lot of personal development, it's likely that the negative thoughts will outweigh the positive ones. These negative thoughts will leak out in some way and stain your body language, your speech and your reactions to other people.

People think about you in whatever way you lead them; you are the leader and they merely follow.

JAY'S STORY:
'I'm Repulsive'

Jay complained that girls found him repulsive. I looked at his physical features and saw a very symmetrical, nice-looking face but I also felt a repulsion. Why did a good-looking guy seem so ugly?

Jay was focusing on all the bad things in his life. His body was slumped forward and he had a scowl on his face. He finished his diatribe of woes by saying, 'I must have done something really bad in this or a past life to deserve this.'

Jay was repulsive because what he was thinking about himself was ugly and hateful.

Every time I begin to get negative or moany I remind myself that this will make me look ugly – and that's not a pretty thought!

Lily is quite an ordinary-looking girl, but she's never short of admirers. She never talks herself down, but spends a lot of time making herself feel special. Before she goes to a party she looks in the mirror and says to herself, 'What would a goddess feel like? How would she be standing? How would she walk?' She hums her favourite tune – *Simply the Best* by Tina Turner. And then she feels great.

She told me that she'd done this recently then she'd walked into the party and locked eyes with a man across the room. Instant mutual attraction. She didn't even speak to him before she left the party, but he tracked her down and asked her out. He said he'd noticed her sparkle as soon as she walked in the door!

WANTING VERSUS BEING DESPERATE

When I ask my clients: 'What do you want?', 90 per cent of them start by saying, 'My problem is ...' and then pour out a list of woes and worries. It's odd that when people are asked what they want they prefer to say what they *don't* want or give reasons why they *can't* have what they want!

How often do you say things to yourself like 'I wish I could meet someone nice *but* ...' and then proceed to find a whole list of reasons why you can't. You say, 'There just aren't any decent people out there!' And then you wonder why you don't find one. The word 'but', by the way, is like the backspace delete key on your computer. It erases everything that went before it!

LET GO OF DESPERATION

The level of desperation you associate with finding a partner will determine how you act. If you worry about your biological clock or being alone, your clock will probably tick even more loudly and you'll spend even more time alone. In my experience the more you focus on something, the more it becomes a reality – and that includes the bad stuff.

The question to ask yourself when you think such thoughts is: 'Am I thinking from 'lack' or am I thinking of how wonderful life is right now and that in this frame of mind anything is possible?'

Awakening Your Natural Self

Enjoying the Benefits

When Mary's partner left her she was miserable for a while until one day she decided that if she was going to be single she might as well take advantage of all the benefits. She started to go out on her own, enjoyed her own company and made sure she had a great time. She told herself that when the time was right, that 'special man' would just appear in her life.

After two years of a super single lifestyle, she suddenly found herself being pursued by two men. Mary knew unconsciously that when you stop searching for something, it seems to appear of its own accord.

If you are wondering why you haven't found the person of your dreams when you've been wanting them to appear for so long, perhaps it's because your thoughts are actually creating barriers to what you really want. Sometimes we do this unconsciously to protect ourselves from being hurt. Then we can sit back smugly and say, 'Of course I knew it would never happen ...'

Do you honestly think that this is the best strategy for having a wonderful life?

CATCHING THOSE RUNAWAY THOUGHTS

Some of us have been taught that thinking negatively is being realistic. I don't agree. What would it be like if you were able to catch those thoughts as they came in and replace them with something positive instead?

LINDA'S STORY:

'Free and Happy'

When Linda left her boyfriend of six years because he wouldn't deal with his angry outbursts, she often found herself thinking about what she missed and then she'd get upset.

When she thought about missing her boyfriend I noticed she looked down and to her left. Most of us have a certain place where we look when we are miserable, worried or down. I asked Linda to deliberately look in the opposite direction. As soon as she did, the negative thoughts seemed to be much weaker.

When I asked Linda what she'd rather be thinking instead, she said, 'I'd like to focus on how nice it feels to be free and happy.'

By learning to focus on the sense of being free and happy without any reference to her ex's anger, Linda's energy concentrated on what she did want and opened another door to the endless possibilities that were just sitting there waiting for her to pick them up.

If you are having negative thoughts it is because you are focusing your energy on something you want *but* don't have, or there is something bad in your life that you want to be free of.

Saying things like 'I wish I was in a relationship' with a longing sad tone is devoting energy to how bad you feel without a relationship. It is very different from thinking about how wonderful it would be to have a relationship with a smile on your face and feeling happy with the way things are right now.

Energy follows thought. What you focus on is what you attract.

The key to working with thoughts is awareness. The more aware you are of when you think negative thoughts and how they make you feel, the easier it is to do something to banish them.

The more you focus on what you want and imagine yourself having that or being like that or re-member how it felt to be extraordinary, special, at one with yourself with a sense that life is great, the more you will attract a life like that.

Catching your Thoughts

- Choose a day and resolve to be 'on the listen-out' for any thoughts that aren't very helpful.
- As you catch each negative thought, notice what your body is doing. If you are slumped, sit up straight and pull your shoulders back. If your legs are crossed, uncross them. If you're looking in a particular direction, look in the opposite direction. You may want to stand up and move around.
- If you are alone, you can brush your hands down your head, your body and your arms and imagine the thoughts sinking down into the earth.

♥ And when you've done that, ask yourself: 'What could I think instead that would create possibilities and make me feel good right now?' Maybe you'd just like to think of how you are when you are at your best and remember that you've had many moments like that in your life and will have many more if you continue to look for them.

Like most new habits, this takes some practice. But once you learn to monitor your thoughts, catch them before they run away with you and then replace them with more positive thoughts, you'll have a much more positive view of life.

YOUR TREE OF PERSONAL POWER

In Chapter 2 we looked at the Eastern concept of energy centres. One of the key components of these philosophies is balance. The explorations that follow are designed to help you get a sense of balance and enhance your personal power. If you do them regularly enough, you may find yourself becoming more of who you are and what you want – and then imagine what amazing relationships you might attract!

Meeting your Needs from Personal Power

There are many areas of life where we would like to get more clarity and feel better about ourselves. What do you want more of?

What Do You Want?	Area of Focus
Do you want to feel really grounded and have a sense of belonging?	**Base of spine**
Do you want to increase your sexual energy and feel more sexually open?	**Sacral area**
Do you want to like yourself more?	**Solar plexus**
Do you want to be more loving or more open to being loved?	**Heart**
Do you want to be more open and honest and stand up for yourself?	**Throat**
Do you want to be more intuitive in your approach to yourself, other people and relationships?	**Between eyebrows**
Do you want to explore your own spirituality or develop more spiritual relationships?	**Crown of head**

Planting your Tree

This exploration is a great way to start the day. If you really want to go to town on it, try doing this somewhere in the open, perhaps in the garden or by flowing water. You could even do it in the shower. Water is very cleansing.

- Before you begin, spend a few moments breathing slowly in and out. Focus on your breath and allow your body to relax.
- Focus your attention on the base of your spine and think of what it is like to be solidly grounded.
- Imagine that roots go through your feet into the earth. Think of the friends you have and those you'd like to make.

- Say to yourself: 'I am allowing myself to have good friends and enjoy socializing and being connected to other people.'
- Place your hand on your belly and imagine you are touching the power centre of your entire being. Imagine your power is a warm red glow. Think of your sexiest moment.
- Say to yourself: 'I am allowing myself to be a truly sexy and desirable person.'
- Gently rest your hand on your solar plexus. Think of your 'This is me' moments. Imagine a small yellow sun spinning inside you, sending out rays and sparks like a Catherine wheel firework.
- Say to yourself: 'I am allowing my true self to shine out on everyone like the sun's rays.'
- Move your hand to your heart and imagine it is covered with fine pink silk that filters in all the good things and keeps out the bad. Think of times when you've felt love or loved someone.
- Say to yourself: 'I am allowing myself to be more loving and to let love into my heart.'
- Now place your fingertips on your throat. Think of all the things you want to express and imagine standing on a mountain saying them all and being your true self.
- Say to yourself: 'I am allowing myself to truly feel and communicate my honest feelings.'
- Move your fingertips to the place between your eyebrows, close your eyes and imagine that you are linked to all the ideas and thoughts out there in the world.
- Say to yourself: 'I am allowing myself to sense other people and pick up their signals.'
- Focus your attention on the top of your head and imagine that you are a very important and essential part of a super system. It's called the world.
- Say to yourself: 'I am allowing myself to connect with the world around me and be part of all the good things in life and contribute my energy to making the world a better place.'
- Finally, place your hands one on top of another on your belly and breathe in and out. As you breathe in, imagine that you are taking the light of the universe all the way into your belly. As you breathe out, imagine all the stuff you don't want going out from the top of your head right down your spine and leaving via the earth.

Do this as often as you want to feel really balanced, energized and peaceful.

This process is the mental equivalent of having a shower after a long day. And it keeps your mental immune system firing on all cylinders!

YOUR RELATIONSHIP LESSONS

Relationships teach you lessons. If you've had a few bummers, then you might be inclined to feel that it's your lot or that it can't get any better. Not true. Instead of feeling sorry for yourself or regretting the past, your job is to accept the lessons, forgive and love the other person. And then think of all that you have learned and ask yourself how you can use your newfound wisdom to make sure you find the love that's right for you.

For example you may realize that in intimate relationships you've often been too willing to do what someone else wanted at the expense of your own desires. Check these patterns against your work history and your relationships with your friends and family. The more learning you do, the more you'll probably realize that the lessons you learn from your intimate relationships can be applied to all areas of your life.

'FAILURE' IS YOUR TEACHER

'Experience allows you to recognize a mistake when you do it again.'

Franklin P. Jones

When a relationship finishes many of us have been trained to look on it as a failure. Those unspoken social rules say that if a relationship doesn't end in marriage and 'happy ever after' then it's failed. What if you thought of it not as a failure but as feedback to help you prepare for something more suitable and fulfilling?

I believe that all the relationships we've had have been sent to us to help us learn the lessons we need to get back in touch with our true selves. Whether a relationship is a quick shag or a 20-year marriage, and whether it appears 'good' or 'bad' at the time, it has much to teach you.

Unfortunately, many of us have to learn the same lesson over and over again, and each time we don't pick up the message, the lesson gets harder.

The Knight in Shining Armour

When I met Alexis, she was in yet another relationship with a man who was very good at meeting her needs – and boy, was she needy! He was a romantic knight in shining armour and she was a weak damsel who wanted someone to pick her up when she fell.

As she developed her self-reliance and confidence, however, she needed less rescuing and less romance. Eventually she realized that her partner was feeding his own need to feel good by helping her, and when she didn't need so much help, he felt bad. After 10 years, she left him.

When I asked Alexis what the lessons were, she realized that she had been in that relationship to learn to be less needy.

She's currently in a relationship that's very different. Her new partner is supportive, not at all jealous, and very spontaneous, but he doesn't go out of his way to pave her path with rose petals and confess his undying love. At first she tried to fit him into the 'living together' box. He didn't want to play. Alexis was launching a new career for herself and had no idea where she would be in two years' time. She realized that while she'd been trying to tie him down, she didn't really want to commit to being tied down herself. She told me that he was a perfect playmate for right now and that whatever happened in the future, she was going to enjoy every moment of what was happening right now.

LOOK BACK AND LEARN ...

'Fall seven times, stand up eight.'
Japanese proverb

When a relationship is ending we are often so caught up in painful emotions that we can't think rationally about it. Often we moan for years. How about stopping the whining and looking for what you got out of it? There may have been some great times or maybe it was just so awful that you had to go. Either way, you learned something from it and that was what you needed to learn in order to move on.

Even a person who leaves an abusive relationship after years of hanging in there has ultimately had the positive experience using their personal power to resist and break free. Even the bad stuff is sent to move us on to somewhere else.

When you look back on your relationships, you may begin to realize how they have all been rich pools of wisdom and self-awareness and you can be grateful for the pleasure *and* the pain. You might not be able to get in touch with all the lessons straightaway. We are not trained to come out of a relationship and say, 'Well, that's over – what did I learn?' But when the anger, blame and battles fade away, we can often look back and celebrate the experience ... and look forward to whatever's next.

LUCINDA'S STORY:
Saving People

Lucinda had recently left a three-month relationship. She told me that very early on in this relationship it had suddenly dawned on her that she was always charging in to save people and always put what she wanted on a back burner while she was on her mission. Sure enough, the woman she'd just left had some serious 'therapy' problems.

Lucinda said that looking back, she'd done the same thing in all of the three meaningful relationships she'd had. So, even though it was difficult for her to resist this woman, she was really determined to break free. She'd learned that this pattern didn't work. She also realized that she wanted a relationship where she was paying as much attention to her own needs as she was to the other person's.

The Relationship Lesson Game

Here's your opportunity to think about your past relationships, remember the positive times, discover the lessons and celebrate. You can make this really fun by acting it out or you can just do it in your head.

Acknowledging the Lessons
Find some space where you have room to move forward and backwards comfortably.

You're going to imagine a line on the ground that represents your life – past, present and future. This is your relationship 'timeline'. Pick a spot somewhere in the middle that seems good enough to represent the present. This is your 'now' spot.

Some people like to think of the past and future running to either side of them. Others prefer to think of the past as running behind them and the future running in front. Do whatever is best for you.

Once you've decided on the direction of your line, you're ready to go.

- Turn round and face the past. Take some time to think about the significant relationships in your past.
- For each relationship, mark out a place on the line either in your head or with a piece of paper. The most recent relationship will be closest to the present.
- Start moving alongside the line in the direction of the past. Stop at the spot that represents the most recent relationship and step into it. Put yourself fully back into your last relationship and run through it. Imagine it as if you are reliving it through your own eyes and ears.
- Ask your unconscious mind to let you know what lessons you gained and what was good about the relationship. Don't think too hard, just do it.
- Step out of the spot and to the side and from a 'rational observer' point of view consider what the lessons were and how you have moved on.
- Then take a moment to remember all the positive moments. And regardless of how you feel, thank that person for being part of your life.
- When you've finished, return to the now spot and acknowledge how the past has helped you be who you are today, even if it is not so perfect *yet*. Take some time to write down what you've learned.

You can repeat the process with all your past relationships. Do you notice any patterns? Was there a lesson it took you a few relationships to learn?

There are some rules to this learning game. If you learn something, you can move on to the next thing. If you don't learn, you stay in the same class and the lessons get harder! The more you know about how it works, the quicker it is to learn and move on.

Integrating the Lessons into the Future

It's useful to look back and learn, but you want a great future too, don't you? You can recognize as many lessons as you've hairs on your head, but if you don't integrate them into how you'll behave in the future, they don't have much point. The next exploration is designed to help you make a better, more positive future.

- ❤ Stand in the 'now' spot and face away from the past towards the future.
- ❤ Step forward into the spot.
- ❤ Imagine yourself relating as your natural self – being honest, liking yourself, being true to yourself and being strong.
- ❤ As you do this, ask yourself:

  'How am I relating?'

  'What might I be doing differently?'

  'How are the lessons of the past helping me?'
- ❤ Finally, look back to the now spot and, knowing what you know of the future, give yourself some advice. It's surprising how wise you can be when you put your mind to it.

UNLEASHING YOUR NATURAL SEXUALITY

YOUR SEXUAL ENERGY: SENDING IT OUT OR SITTING ON IT

Sexual energy is the most primal and powerful drive in the human psyche. Some people let it flow freely while others sit on it in an attempt to keep it from surfacing. Whether you are single and searching or have been married for years, setting your sexual energy free can be a very empowering act and good fun too!

SAM'S STORY:
Best Friend

Sam came to see me because, like many of my clients, he wasn't getting beyond the best friend stage with girls. He was a nice enough guy and quite good-looking. I asked him what he said to himself when he saw an attractive girl. He thought for a while and said, 'She's quite presentable. I'd like to talk to her.'

I looked him straight in the eye and said with a smile, 'You're a *big* liar. What do you *really* think?'

Sam pulled back a little, then gave a naughty smile as he said in a much sexier voice, 'Mmmm, what I'm really thinking is: "I could do *that* some damage!"' Of course this is just a colloquial term and doesn't mean he wanted to hurt her. He just had a fleeting full-bodied sense of the primal urge of powerful sex. And when he said that I was really aware of the tremendous sexual energy he was giving off.

When you see someone attractive, it's perfectly natural to feel a strong lusty sense of sexual desire. But some people, like Sam, censor their natural thoughts. Censoring thoughts censors the energy – energy follows thought. So, if you don't think sexy, you won't act sexy!

While I was running with my boyfriend, who was wearing tight Lycra shorts, a girl walked past and gave him the full up-and-down look. 'Did you see that?' he said incredulously. 'She was staring straight at my "lunchbox"!' 'Yes,' I grinned, 'women do that too!'

If you are a naturally sexy woman, you'll agree that we are just as likely to eye up an attractive person and check out their bodies as men are. Sadly, many of us have been rigorously trained not to do this. And as a result we aren't sending out those sexy vibes.

In some cultures, men are trained not to look either – or not to make it obvious!

NICOLE'S STORY:
'Am I Really Attractive?'

Nicole called me because she wanted to tell me what it was like being a Frenchwoman in London. She laughed, 'Since I've been here, I've been wondering just how attractive I really am!'

When she lived in Paris, Nicole was used to men looking her up and down appreciatively and smiling and passing by. Some of them made approaches and some didn't. Either way, she said that it made her feel attractive and desirable.

When she came to London, men just didn't look at her. Although she was quite self-confident, she admitted that at times she wondered what was wrong with her. And then she'd realized it wasn't her, it was that British men have generally been trained not to look because it's not 'proper'. Baloney!

From my experience, many American and some European men don't look either. This has to do with cultural conditioning. Men have learned it's somehow not 'right' to look at women like that. When they do do it, they make sure that women can't catch them at it! But if a woman doesn't notice a man looking, she won't pick up on his sexual vibes.

MANUEL'S STORY:
The Melting Look

At the end of my flirting courses I line the men up on one side of the room and the women on the other. Both groups are asked to walk down the line of the opposite sex and look every person up and down in as sexy a way as they want to. When I announce what we are going to do, there's an atmosphere of shock and fear and embarrassed giggles. On the first round many people are just too 'polite' to give 'the look'.

Manuel was different. He was a Brazilian who had come on the course because he felt uncomfortable about flirting in the Brazilian way with women in the UK. He didn't take long to relearn his natural style. As he walked down the line looking at the women, in turn each one started to quiver, wiggle and squeal! One of them said later, 'I felt as though he was melting me with that look.'

Manuel was just a very ordinary-looking guy, but he knew how to let his natural sexuality rise up and come out of his eyes, his smile and his whole body. As he did that he was directly transmitting sexual energy to the women and they were physically affected by the vibes! Manuel grew up in a culture that encouraged open sexuality.

We all have huge sexual energy, we just haven't learned how to unleash it. Stick with me, because that's about to change!

SENSING YOUR SEXUALITY

Before you can send out sexual vibes, you have to have a strong sense of your own sexuality.

Everyone expresses their sexuality in different ways. You might have a very visual sense, be acutely aware of looks and colour and able to visualize things easily. You may be more auditory, in which case sounds and what people say are important to you. Or maybe you're a touchy feely person who gets a feel for things and notices physical sensations.

We all use all our senses, but we often have one that is dominant. The following exploration is designed for you to 'get a sense' of your sexuality and notice which sense is predominant for you.

Sensing your Sensuality

💜 Create a sexy atmosphere: light candles, burn aromatic oils, play loud rock music, wear a nappy – whatever turns you on.

💜 Lie, stand or sit comfortably in whatever position allows you to get most turned on.

💜 Take some time to remember your most erotic moments. If they're ones you have had with yourself, play them out. If they're ones you have had with other people, recall the experience and get as turned on as you want. By all means do whatever you feel the urge to do, but don't allow yourself to come before you've gone through as many experiences as you want!

It helps to recall different phases of the sexual cycle. You will probably discover that you have different needs and desires as you progress through the stages. Remember a time when:

You were not being sexual with a lover but something happened and you got turned on.
You were indulging in gentle foreplay.
You were in the heat of passion.

Get in Touch with the Feelings

Remember where you enjoyed being touched or touching yourself. Pay attention to the detail of the touch. Was it rough or gentle, slow or fast? Where was it specifically? Did it start somewhere and finish somewhere else? Did you need breaks in between or was it a continuous movement? Really be aware of how it felt. Were you lying or sitting or bending over? Were you wearing something that felt good? Is there material through which you like to be touched?

Notice the visual aspects that made it richer. Was there something good about the décor? What about the way the other person looked at you? Were you making long deep eye contact? Did you see images in your head? Were you wearing something that looked great? Was the other person? Was there something special about the colour, the style, the fit?

What about the sounds? Were there words that really turned you on? What was it about them – the words themselves, the tone, volume, rhythm, speed, the type of voice? Maybe they were said into your ear or you felt them through another part of your body. What words really turn you on? Are there particular times when you like to hear these words? Was there some music or other sound going on that added to the excitement?

How about smell? Is there a particular smell that turns you on – perfume or flowers or petrol or newly mown grass? Is there something about your partner's smell that you love – the smell of a particular part of their body or of their mouth as they go to kiss you?

Sex can be very tasty too. Do you like the taste of melted chocolate on his penis or strawberry lip gloss on her nipples? Maybe you like the taste of a certain part of their body, or your own. Or maybe there's something you like to eat while you're having sex. Do you like to have your partner blindfold you and feed you fruit or drip champagne into your mouth? (Beware of putting alcohol on your genitals, it burns like hell!) Again, your taste is unique!

Mapping your Sexuality

Your sensory sexual needs are only a small part of your unique sexual map. You have all kinds of preferences, some of which you're very aware of and some you might not know about yet.

Are there things that you absolutely love? Are there things that you haven't tried yet but would like to? What would you never do? And what are you going to do about getting what you want?

The map below will help you to figure out your own sexuality. I've given you a few categories and some suggestions to start you thinking. Add your own categories and comments and enjoy yourself!

Category	What I Like	What I'd Like to Try	What I Don't Like	Action
Locations Where do you like to have sex – which rooms in the house, indoors, outdoors, where you are likely to be discovered, in public places, high up, in the sea?				
Timing Morning, evening, afternoon, the middle of the night? After something, during something, before something? Quickies or long slow sex?				

Category	What I Like	What I'd Like to Try	What I Don't Like	Action
Props and People Consider sex toys, other people together with or in addition to your lover, clothing for you and for them. What else?				
Fantasies What are they? Are there any you'd like to come true? What factors might affect them in reality? Which ones are you happy to keep in the realm of fantasy?				
Giving What are you prepared to do for someone else? What turns you on about that?				

BEING A VERY SEXY PERSON

If you're thinking, 'How can I be sexy?', *stop*. Change that question to: 'How can I open out and expand my sexy side?' The first thought suggests sexuality is something you learn. It's not. You already have it. It may be that you just aren't aware of it or are holding it back. You can set your sexuality free and let sexiness run through you all the time.

Being sexy isn't the same thing as feeling horny. Being sexy is a state of mind based on the premise that you are a sexual being. It means that you feel sexy, you act sexy and you look sexy. Being sexy is about loving your own body and being very happy with your sexuality. You're sexy when you can look in the mirror and think, 'Oooh ...'

Many of us are not as comfortable with our bodies and sexuality as we could be. We are still bound by the ties of our sexual inheritance, according to Richard Craze, author of *A Beginner's Guide to Tantric Sexuality*:

'As human beings we are bound up with guilt and embarrassment about our sexuality. This is part of our upbringing, especially if we've been brought up in the West. We are the inheritors of two thousand years of sexual bigotry and repression.'

And when you've not been in a relationship for a while, it's easy to let your sexual energy levels sink to an all-time low. Because of the ridiculous idea that some people have that masturbation is second rate compared to sex with someone else, you may feel as if you're missing out. When you feel like that, you will give out a measure of desperate energy.

Learning to be a sexual human being all the time and loving sex with yourself as much as with someone else will boost your sexual energy levels and replace the 'I'm desperate for sex' vibes with 'I'm a very sexy person' vibes.

Generating Sexual Energy

Many of the Eastern energy disciplines like chi kung, tai chi and martial arts focus on the sacral area, the centre of sexual energy. This is also the centre of personal power. What a wonderful combination. They use breathing and focus to generate energy in that area. With the help of your imagination, you can link this energy to your sexuality and run it all round your body. And it feels great.

Warm Up Exercise
- ❤ Stand with your feet about 30 cm apart. Slightly bend your knees and place the backs of your wrist in your kidney area on either side of your back.
- ❤ Start to make circular movements with your hips going first from right to left and then repeating the same number of movements from left to right.
- ❤ As you do this, focus your mind on the sacral area about two inches below your belly button. You might even want to chant something to yourself. I like the words from George Michael's song *I want your sex.*
- ❤ Enjoy it.

Now you're ready to whip up some sexual energy!

Generating Energy ...
- ❤ Stand in a place where you have some space to stretch out and lie down.
- ❤ Stand with your feet hip-width apart. Keep your hands at your sides and let your shoulders drop comfortably. Place your tongue on the roof of your mouth (this helps the energy to circulate).
- ❤ Breathe in gently through your nose and as you do so imagine your breath going to your belly. When you breathe in, your diaphragm pushes down and your lungs expand downwards and outwards. Your belly expands, pushing downwards and outwards. When you breathe out, your diaphragm pushes up, expelling the air from your lungs. When you get a sense of this it's easier to breathe correctly.
- ❤ As you breathe in, imagine you are breathing in lots of light and sunshine and that it whooshes into your belly, expanding it and moving slowly up your spine to the top of your head. Feel the tingle in your vertebrae as it moves upwards.
- ❤ As you breathe out, imagine you are breathing the light and sunshine round slowly from the top of your head down to your belly again. It's like breathing in a circle. Learning to breathe like this is the basis for being able to practise chi kung, tai chi or tantric sex.
- ❤ Continue breathing this way until you feel it is natural and comfortable. Feel the energy circulate. Now you're ready for the juicy bit.

- Begin to massage your genitals in a very slow and teasing way and as you notice your excitement starting, be aware of where it starts. Stop and put your hands back down by your sides.
- As you breathe in, imagine this excitement (your sexual energy) is travelling up your spine and back down again to the sacral area. If necessary, excite yourself some more. Do this very slowly. Stop and repeat.
- As your sexual energy rises and expands, ask yourself which animal or natural element symbolizes the way you feel right now and why. (Animals are a good choice because they don't know the meaning of the words 'better not', they just answer the call of their sexuality.)
- Imagine you are this animal or whatever symbol you choose and allow your sexual energy to expand freely.
- Think of what you'd like to say to yourself that affirms you are a very sexy person.
- When you have a strong sense of your sexual energy, you can allow it to subside and know that it's waiting to rise up and fill your entire body any time you want.
- This animal can become your trigger idea for generating sexuality. Each time you think of the animal you should begin to feel a slight sexual tremor. (Don't worry, no one else will be able to see this – they'll just notice you are sort of sexy!)
- The next stage is to practise this without touching yourself. Use fantasies, porn, your animal trigger, your special sexy affirmation or whatever it takes to get you going.

If the old ideas about your sexuality return, do the breathing exercise and say your affirmation to yourself. Faced with such a powerful energy, your conditioning will soon disappear! And you can move on to an even more juicy exploration ...

A Very Saucy Method to Enhance your Power

It's interesting that your sexual energy centre is also linked to your personal power centre. What would it be like if you could link a sense of how you want to be with the feeling of orgasm? I can assure you it's mindblowingly powerful! And it's quite simple to do:

- Set a sexy and exciting scene, stand or sit comfortably and relax.
- Focus your mind on your sacral area, in the middle of your belly. Think of how you are at your best – get a real sense of it using your animal or word trigger.
- Start to masturbate. Take it long and slow, build yourself up to almost having an orgasm and then stop.
- As you inhale, imagine those sensations rising up your spine, and as they do, imagine the sense of how you are at your best rising up your spine too.
- Repeat the stop–start stuff until you can't hold out any more.
- Then as you begin to go for it for the last time, take a moment or two to think of your personal power, how you are when you are really your true self, and then let yourself come … and feel the power running through you with each orgasmic pulsation … and imagine it exploding out into the world … taking you with it.

Use this exploration as a way of enhancing anything you want to visualize for yourself. Imagine the relationship, job, home or whatever you want in your life and let it come into you and explode through your sexuality out into the world. Do this as often as you want to feel sexy, powerful and utterly amazing.

Someone once said, 'The best sex I've ever had is with myself.' Most of us have been programmed to believe that the most fulfilling sex is the sex we have with a partner. I'm not so sure.

Great sexual experiences aren't just for people in a relationship, they're possible for everyone. My friend Leora invited me to an introductory evening in tantric sex. I was pleased to see that almost half the participants were single people. They'd obviously decided that they weren't going to wait until they found the 'perfect' partner before they learned to get the most out of their sexuality. And imagine how prepared they are going to be for mindblowing sex when they *do* find someone they like. (For more details on tantra classes in the UK, *see* the Resources section at the back of this book.)

And now, being your sexy, powerful self, aware of the lessons of the past and looking ahead to the future, let's have a look at some cool skills that will enhance your ability to relate in a more natural way.

CHAPTER 5

LOVING, CLARIFYING AND CONNECTING

'The shoe that fits one person pinches another; there is no recipe for living that suits all cases. Each of us carries his own unique life form – which cannot be used by any other.'
Carl Jung

From the very first encounter with another person you become co-architects and builders of your relationship. That relationship may last one night or one lifetime, but you are on a journey together and you cannot know where or how it will end.

Because these journeys take place as we are growing up and learning our life lessons, we seem to generate situations that are ripe for our personal lessons, the ones that move us on and help us to develop.

If you want to really attract the kind of love that's right for you, you have to learn to love yourself as much as you expect someone else to. And if you want to know what's really right for you, it's important to clarify what you believe and value so that you don't end up with what you don't want! And eventually you are going to connect with people and you will want to be best equipped to discover as much as you can about them and deepen those connections.

LOVING

LOVING YOURSELF

'You, yourself, as much as anybody in the entire universe, deserve your love and affection.'

Buddha

There's no question about it, loving yourself is very, very important to your well-being and your ability to attract the love you want. People who can't love themselves may find it difficult to love anyone else and they don't easily attract love. If you don't love yourself, you may either send out a message that says, 'Please give me love because I haven't got enough for myself,' or drown someone with love in the hope that they will stay with you and feed your need for love, or put up a barrier that says: 'Don't love me – I'm not love-able enough.'

What if you were to send out messages like these:

'Here is my love as a gift to you and I expect nothing in return.'
'I'm so love-able.'

What might that do to a person who's attracted to you?

YOU DON'T HAVE TO BE PERFECT

'We're never so vulnerable as when we trust someone – but paradoxically, if we cannot trust, neither can we find love or joy.'

Walter Anderson

ELAINE'S STORY:
'I Never Burden Them ...'

Elaine is very concerned about what people will think of her. She is also very kind to people. She couldn't understand why one of her friends had turned on her. She said, 'I never burden her with my problems.' And she didn't. She was so concerned to appear perfect that she held back a lot and then wondered why people resented her.

People are suspicious of people who appear to be without flaws. You don't have to go on and on about your problems but admitting that you have flaws and problems like everyone else indicates that you too are human. Elaine's friends couldn't connect with her because she put on an appearance of being perfect superwoman.

Are you trying too hard to be perfect? Or are you prepared to admit you're human and you don't always get it right? How liberating might that be?

I'm not suggesting you spill all the beans at once. Sometimes we feel the need to hold back information because it's not appropriate or relevant or a person isn't ready for it yet. But there's a difference between holding back out of fear of exposing yourself and holding back because you want to take it slowly and not overwhelm someone.

REVEALING YOURSELF

'These are the parts of you that must be communicated if you are going to be known. Otherwise, please back off and review your motives ...'
Dr Neil Warren

We've already worked on what's great about you and I hope you're beginning to feel OK about spreading the good news to other people. But as well as the good stuff, we've all got things that we're scared someone will find out about. Everyone's closet has a skeleton or two.

VERONICA'S STORY:
To Tell or Not to Tell

Veronica told me that she'd done some nude photographs for a less than respectable magazine in what she called 'another life' when she was in desperate financial trouble. She was worried that any future boyfriend might reject her if he found out.

I suggested that if she was going to have a committed relationship she would have to decide whether to keep the secret or make a clean break and share this part of her past.

There are two choices here. Keeping the secret means always living in fear that someone will find out. And if they do find out via the jungle telegraph, they may feel disappointed or get the feeling that you've lied to them. Being open about whatever it is can be cleansing, especially if it was in another life. I always remind clients that Jesus was very fond of Mary Magdalene, who was a fallen woman made good. Everyone can change and it's how we handle what we've done that makes the difference between rejection and acceptance.

Veronica decided that she would like to come clean about her past. I suggested that she might not want to share this on a first date and that she should find an appropriate moment in the relationship, not so soon as to put the other person off, but before too much commitment has been made.

What would you be prepared to reveal to someone and what do you want to hide? The following exploration is designed to help you get a feel for what's keeping you from being totally open.

What Are You Prepared to Reveal?

- Make a list of your secrets, faults, hopes, despairs and challenges. What health issues, food likes and dislikes and quirky habits do you have? (Yes, include them even if they are disgusting!)
- Go through each one and do a feeling check.
- If there are things you register as 'Couldn't ever tell anyone that', what value do you get from keeping those secrets? What do you think would happen if you let some of them out?
- If you are already in a relationship, ask yourself what you currently hide from your partner. It might be having a few more drinks than you're prepared to admit to. It might be wearing something they wouldn't approve of. The idea is to think about how honest you are being with yourself and how much of your true self you are hiding.

You have to make the choice here. But remember, the more people you are open with, the more support you're going to have if your secret does come out. You can always turn to whoever is nasty enough to expose you and say confidently, 'But that's old news. I thought *everyone* knew that.'

LOVING OTHERS

'Love isn't about finding someone perfect; it's about learning to love an imperfect person perfectly.'

Author unknown

LETTING OTHERS BE

When you really want to connect with another person it may seem a strange idea to let them be. We're usually full of suggestions as to what other people ought to do in order to make us happier. We're always reminding them how dismally they've failed to meet our needs. And we give them lessons in how to improve:

> 'If only you'd ring me once a day, I'd know you loved me.'
> 'Why can't you be more romantic and send me flowers more often?'
> 'If you loved me, you'd stop drinking.'

It's all 'me, me, me'.

And when they don't change, probably because they don't want to or are not ready to, we don't give up. We have some great tactics for steamrollering change. We nag, cry, instil guilt and generally do whatever we think it takes. And sometimes the other person just refuses outright. If they're more cowardly, they may try temporarily and if they do want to make the change, they will, and if they don't, chances are they'll revert right back to their old ways.

SIMON'S STORY:
'Heal Thyself'

Simon went on a personal development course and returned home full of the stuff he'd learned. He spent the next two weeks amateurishly using his newfound skills on his wife. Then one day she told him she was fed up with being treated like a therapy client.

He remembered the words 'Physician, heal thyself' and realized that the only way he could influence his wife was to continue to work on himself and trust she'd notice the changes in him.

About eight months later she said to him, 'You've changed so much I'm impressed. I'd like to find out more about what it is you're doing, because it obviously works!'

You can't force change on someone, so the best thing to do is to pay attention to your own growth, be your best self and see what they pick up. (This doesn't mean that you can't influence them in many ways with subtle conversational tactics. You'll find out more about how to do that in the next chapter ...) If they are ready, they'll see something working for you and want to know how they can get results too.

I reckon that if they aren't ready, they aren't ready. And you have the choice: leave them or leave them be. (If you want to work on loving someone by leaving them be, there's a great exercise in the next section.)

GODS AND GURUS EVERY ONE

Everyone you meet is different. A black friend of mine once ran a workshop called 'Celebrate the Difference'. Through a series of eye-opening processes he led his mainly white audience to understand that instead of trying to pretend we are all the same, we should value the difference. Difference is a great lesson. It confronts us and says, 'Are you going to be open to new ways and ideas or are you going to cling to what you've always known?'

Everyone you meet has some valuable idea or skill or way of looking at the world that can enrich you. Sometimes you see it and want it and at other times you realize it's a lesson in how *not* to be. Either way, you are learning.

There's an old tantric concept that everyone is really a god. Even if this sounds far-fetched, it can be a really fun game to look at your partner or friends in this way. If they were a god or goddess, or a guru, what would be their speciality?

My boyfriend would be the god of historical knowledge and my guru of motorcycling. My friend Lesley would be the goddess of canapés and caring. My brother would be the god of humour because he's such a great mimic and a genius at making up witty songs about people and he'd be my sensible guru as well, and my friend Judith would be the goddess of succeeding in the face of adversity.

GILLIAN'S STORY:
Boyfriend from Hell

Gillian came to see me because she couldn't make up her mind about leaving her man. Her friends called him 'the boyfriend from hell'. He was not at all romantic, he was very untidy and on top of that he had made it clear he didn't want to live with Gillian. She ran through a whole host of complaints about the guy and finished by telling me how no matter what she did, he just didn't match up to her ideal – though he did have some wonderful qualities and if only he could work on the other stuff he'd be Mr Perfect.

I asked Gillian to focus first on her own life and what she hoped to achieve. She started to talk about all the things she wanted to do and her plans to open an alternative health centre and the strong feeling she kept getting about being drawn to the States. I asked her whether settling down with one man was right for her right now. She laughed when she realized that she was as much a free spirit as he was. I then asked her to focus on what she liked about him. She smiled as she talked about their shared values, similar beliefs and background and sense of adventure and fun that was second to none. She realized that he was just what she needed at the moment.

After she'd done the exploration, I told her to go home and sit quietly with her man and look at him whilst she focused on all the things she liked. I suggested that she should just spend some time loving him for who he was rather than resenting him for who he was not.

In our next session Gillian told me that as she had done this she began to feel a deep sense of love directly in her sacral area, the place where she sensed sexual excitement, but it was actually a stronger, less sexual and more solid feeling. As a result, she realized that this man was wonderful for now and that just as she couldn't predict her own future right now, neither could she predict the future of her relationship.

Sometimes it's so easy to focus on someone's bad qualities that we forget what it was that we were first attracted to. And sometimes we need to search for the good to learn that maybe there just isn't enough there to warrant continuing the relationship.

The next exploration is designed to help you open out to the positive aspects of someone with whom you are in an intimate relationship. And if you're not, use it on your friends. You never know what hidden depths you might find – and if you truly can't find anything worth hanging on to, then at least you can say you looked before you left!

What's Great about Them?

Focus your mind on your heart centre and imagine connecting to the heart of the person you are checking out.

- ♥ What do you really like about this person? What positive qualities do they have? If negative qualities come up at this point, just acknowledge that they exist and continue your search for the good stuff.
- ♥ What qualities do you like in them that you don't have? How can that benefit you?
- ♥ If you notice any negative qualities, are they a reflection of how you are sometimes? (Be honest here!)
- ♥ Assuming you can't change anything, on balance does the positive outweigh the negative or vice versa?

If you feel more positive about the person now, make sure you communicate that to them. Imagine there's a hotline from your heart to theirs and just look at them. Do this often.

And when they irritate you or do things you don't like, try looking at them and thinking, 'They're a human being with flaws just like me,' *and smile.*

CLARIFYING

BIG TOPIC BELIEFS

If you are going to create a truly natural and honest relationship with someone, then you need to be clear about what both of you believe and value.

'Marriage', 'commitment', 'love' and 'for ever and ever', for example, are concepts about which we all have fairly strong opinions. If you ask six people to write down the first six words that come into their mind when they think of these big topics, the chances are they'll come up with many different words and that very few of these will be shared by the entire group. Don't take my word for it. Try it with your friends or your lover.

Eventually these topics are going to crop up in your relationships. Your beliefs about them are going to determine how you behave and will also indicate how you expect the significant other to behave.

Some of your beliefs might be ones you've inherited and might not want. Are you absolutely sure that what you think you want is really what you want? Remember your personal conditioning patterns? If you are going to find the relationship that is really right for you, you may have to discard some of the ready-planned recipes and be creative.

Your life, your choice ...

FOR EVER AND EVER?

From a very early age most of us learn that one day we will meet 'the one' and when we do we will live in bliss together 'till death us do part'. Yet current statistics suggest that over 40 per cent of all marriages end in divorce. It's obvious that relationships are not working out the way they are 'supposed to' and that they don't come with a lifetime guarantee.

Most people say that you have to 'work on a relationship', and to some extent that's very true. But sometimes things come up that you can't work on or compromise. You just want something that the other person doesn't and you have to make your choice.

Many of us haven't found our life purpose at the age of 20 or even 50. And it's perfectly natural that what you wanted at 20 might not be what's right for you at 50. When you first meet someone you like, it's as if you are two colours that appear to match and blend. And then when one or both of the colours begins to change, you could be in for an almighty clash.

And for some people for ever and ever *does* work.

TINA AND ED'S STORY:
Shared Dreams

Tina and Ed are simple souls from very similar backgrounds. Ed runs his own building firm and Tina used to work full time until she had children. They married young. Ed worked very hard to build up his business. They bought and renovated their first house shortly after they got married. Tina enjoyed staying at home with the children and became very involved in community activities. Now the children are older, Tina is setting up her own business and Ed is supporting her.

This is a true white picket fence story. Tina and Ed found they had common dreams and a very strong sense of family values. Both of them are happy with their lives and haven't changed much since they were teenagers.

BARNEY AND ALICE'S STORY:
Separate Dreams

Barney and Alice met at university. They were both ambitious and had dreams of success. Alice always expected that she would eventually have children and give up work to look after them while Barney supported the family.

Barney was a successful lawyer, but he wasn't happy in his work. He'd fallen into the trap of following his parents' dreams and after 10 years he realized that the law was not for him. He decided he wanted to give it all up and become a potter.

Whilst he was perfectly happy to live a simple life, this was not what Alice had planned. She had married a potentially successful lawyer and liked the life that went with that. She was disappointed to find that Barney was rapidly becoming someone else.

Barney and Alice started out with what they thought was the same dream, but unlike Tina and Ed, as they matured they grew in different directions and their dreams were just not compatible.

Before you embark on the 'for ever and ever' boat, it might be a good idea to be clear about what you want and to have a contingency plan for the fact that you might change – radically. Is it really possible to decide now how your life will be in 20 years' time? I know we've been taught to make a life plan, but in many cases these plans turn out to be the ties that bind.

How easy would it be to say to someone, 'I love you now and want to be with you and I can't say how I'll feel tomorrow because I'm still finding out about myself and what I want to be doing'?

BEST FRIEND OR SPECIAL FRIEND?

I've been running a relationship survey on the internet for over a year and have had thousands of replies. One of the questions I asked was: 'What do you want from a partner?'

Some people said they wanted that person to be everything to them and hoped that they would be everything to that person. There was a really strong tendency to use very powerful emotionally charged words like that. And a whole load of them said that they wanted their partner to be the person they would share all their dreams and triumphs with, the person who would shoulder all their problems, their 'best friend'.

Many of us are brought up to believe that a relationship should be all-encompassing and that the ideal relationship is one where most if not all of life's satisfactions come from the partner or from being with that partner.

When you think about it, this is one hell of a demand to make of a person.

RUTH'S STORY:
My Best Friend

Whenever the going got tough for Ruth, her first instinct was to call up hubby for sympathy, because she believed that husbands ought to be best friends too.

At first she used to complain that he didn't listen and wasn't very good at dishing out the sympathy. Then one day a friend said to her, 'Why bother calling him when I'm here? You can talk to me anytime.' Now when Ruth is feeling down or needs a boost, she calls her friends.

Ruth married her husband because they share a lot of values and have fun together. Once she took the pressure off him to be her 'best friend', she had nothing to complain about and could make the most of all the things she enjoys doing with him.

JOHN AND LAURA'S STORY:
Best Friends

John and Laura have been married for 30 years. They were childhood sweethearts. They run a business together and socialize together and meditate together. John tells me that he could count on one hand the number of days they've spent apart. They are very happy. They are each other's best friend. This works for them.

If you're in a relationship where you're expecting someone to be your best friend and you theirs, you might want to think about this:

> If they join in an activity that you love, are they enjoying it or are they doing it reluctantly because they're trying to make you happy?
>
> If there are interests you love but they don't, can you be happy to find another friend to share this activity with and for your partner to do likewise?

PETE AND JACKIE'S STORY:
Special Projects

Like John and Laura, Pete and Jackie have been married for a long time. They too were childhood sweethearts. Pete's international consultancy business has taken him away for long periods of their marriage. Jackie has always been active running her own successful writing career and bringing up their three children. She rarely socializes with her husband because 'socializing with Pete doesn't work'. She has separate interests and friends, but she also works with her husband on special projects. They spend long periods of time apart and long periods of time working closely together. This works for them.

Is it worth considering that it's possible to have a long and healthy relationship with someone and *not* be everything to them? How much easier might it be to sustain that relationship? The following exploration will give you something to think about.

Alternative Resourcing

What qualities *must* a partner have for you? Make a list of the things you think you want. Then go through it and ask these questions:

- ❤ What would happen if your partner didn't have some of these qualities?
- ❤ Which ones must they absolutely have for you to be happy?
- ❤ What would happen if they didn't have these qualities?
- ❤ In the middle of a blank piece of paper draw a symbol to represent yourself. Draw a circle round that symbol. In the space closest to the circle write the names of those people who are dearest to you and who have been very valuable in your life.

- ♥ What items from your 'want list' can be met by the people on this list? Write them down beside their names.
- ♥ And remember that instead of expecting one person to do it all, you have a whole host of people to draw on.

CHILDREN: AN AWESOME RESPONSIBILITY

I believe that the biggest commitment you can make with another person is to bring a child into the world. It amazes me that so many people take so lightly one of the most awesomely responsible tasks you will ever undertake. You are consciously choosing to create new life and take on all the accountability that comes with that.

I'm sure that if you want children you know that the best way to allow them to become themselves and follow their destiny is to set the same example. Before you think about having children you might ask yourself: 'Have I brought myself up to a level where I can take on responsibility for someone else? How might my "stuff" affect a child? What do I need to work on for the sake of my child?'

JENNY AND KIERAN'S STORY:
'It Just Happened'

Jenny and Kieran got married in their early twenties. They had two kids almost immediately, because it 'just happened'. As Kieran admits, 'I suppose having children is expected when you're married.' But Kieran and Jenny didn't stay married long and the kids were put through a very messy divorce.

It amazes me that scores of people don't plan their families, but just let nature take its course. If you want to have children with a partner, it might be useful to check that they have a similar outlook where children are concerned. Above all, I believe it's vital to check both your motives and readiness to take on this awesome responsibility. It could save a lot of heartache later.

And if you don't want children or can't have them, remember that fulfilment of the mother/father/nurturer role can be found in many different ways.

To further explore this subject with or without a partner, check out the relationship survey at the back of this book.

MARRIAGE: THE ULTIMATE GOAL?

'The point of life is not to be married or single – it is to be. We are ... humans being. It does not matter so much what lifestyle we choose – it's what we make of the opportunities to grow that counts.'

Alan Cohen

As I write this I've just been invited to a wedding by two people who met on one of my courses. Agnes had called me six months previously to announce that she and Mark had moved in with each other. She'd told me that the relationship was wonderful and I was very happy for her. Now I'm wondering why I am more excited about them getting married than their moving in together. I realize that I too have been programmed with the idea that marriage is the ultimate goal.

I believe that the harder it is to get out of something, the more committed people have to be before they'll enter into it. With the easy divorce laws most countries are adopting, marriage is now almost as easy to get out of as it is to get into. So how come most people see it as the ultimate commitment? If two people are committed enough to pool their finances and buy a joint property, that's a much bigger bind because it's so much harder to get out of! And as for having a child, splitting up a unit that the child has come to know and is still dependent on is a massive decision.

TRADITIONAL MARRIAGE THOUGHTS

I was 23 when my live-in boyfriend came back from a family visit with an engagement ring and proposed. I was so excited by the idea of being married, I said yes. A few months before the wedding I thought, 'How can I marry someone who questions why I read so many books?' Sometimes we become marriage fans without really knowing what it means to us.

PENNY AND ROBERT'S STORY:
'Keeping Her Happy'

Penny and Robert had been together for five years. Penny had no desire to work and Robert was quite willing to keep her. Penny got the big white church wedding she'd set her heart on, but Robert ran around with just as many women after his marriage as he did before.

To Penny, marriage meant she'd claimed her 'provider'. To Robert, it was just like giving her a car or some money. He did it to keep her happy.

My money says that this marriage won't make the five-year mark.

SOUL MATES BUT NOT SEX MATES

Do you believe there is one special all-singing, all-dancing soul mate waiting for you? Have you considered that it's possible to have many soul mates and that they can take on many different forms? I think it is. How about you? If you did believe this, what new possibilities might it open out for you?

ZANA AND DAVID'S STORY:
Soul Mates

Zana met David on an animal conservation trip to Africa. They shared many dreams about their work and the things they could do together. They were attracted to each other, but nothing happened.

Two years later Zana visited David whilst on a trip to the States. Their friendship deepened and they planned a project together. When she returned home she decided that she valued the friendship enough to let go of wanting him. She said, 'He is a soul mate, even if we aren't meant to be together in the traditional way.'

Zana believes David is one of the many very special soul mates she'll meet along her way.

TAMMY'S STORY:
Sex Mates

Tammy is a 47-year-old attractive, successful single. She travels all over the country and absolutely loves her work. She has a rich and full social life, a fast car and two cats. She's very happy except for one thing. She misses sex.

Tammy doesn't want a full-on relationship because she doesn't want to commit a serious chunk of time to one man. What she does want is to have sex with someone who is reliable, caring and very sensual. Tammy told me that what she wants is a weekend sex mate.

MARRIED AND HAVING FUN
FRANÇOISE AND TOBY'S STORY:
The Conventional Marriage?

Françoise and Toby were married for 49 years. To everyone around them they were a very happy couple in a conventional marriage.

They were happy, but their marriage wasn't always quite so conventional. Toby's sex drive wasn't as high as Françoise's, so for over 20 years she had a lover whom she saw once a week. Their sex life continued with the same excited frenzy until Toby and Françoise retired to France. Françoise was fine about giving up her lover and she and Toby continued to live happily together until his death at the age of 78.

Before you condemn ways of relating that seem unconventional to you, check out what you really want and ask yourself. 'Is there another way for me?' Please don't follow convention just because you think that's what you 'ought' to do.

I'm not saying marriage is right or wrong. I am asking you to think seriously about whether it's the *only* way for you. Sometimes there is another way.

You may find that the questions in the relationship survey in the appendix will help you sound out what you want.

MONOGAMY AND FIDELITY
WHAT'S YOUR TAKE?

This really is a hot topic. Most people expect to have a monogamous relationship and yet in survey after survey over half the men and women in relationships admit to having affairs. What is this telling us? Are our expectations unrealistic?

I was talking to a married Frenchwoman recently. She said, 'I expect that in 10 years' time my husband will have a mistress and I will be very happy for him even if I am a little jealous.' She was smiling as she said it. She thought that marriages were more likely to last if the husband could have his bit of fun! Interesting viewpoint?

Somewhere along the line, however, most of us have learned the rule that fidelity is a sign that everything is alright and that infidelity is a sign that something is wrong.

UNSPOKEN RULES
LIN'S STORY:
'He Shouldn't Want Anyone Else'

Lin had been dating Jarvis for six months. When he looked at another woman, she got very jealous. She said, 'He's with me, so he shouldn't want anyone else. If he goes with someone else, that's it. He's not for me.'

Jarvis did go with someone else, at a stag weekend, and told Lin. Lin dropped him immediately. She was furious.

When I asked Lin if she and Jarvis had ever discussed monogamy or made any promises, she reluctantly had to admit that they hadn't. And yet she expected him to stick to an unwritten, undiscussed and unagreed rule.

We may think that because we are having sex with someone regularly we are automatically entitled to fidelity. There seems to be an unspoken rule that after a certain undefined time, sexual monogamy just happens. Yet men are not naturally monogamous and it seems, according to some surveys, that women aren't either.

A lover may whisper in a moment of passion, 'You're the only one for me,' and it's taken as a commitment to fidelity. People make marriage vows to 'forsake all others'. But it's all very vague. I think couples might benefit from some in-depth discussions about what 'fidelity' and 'monogamy' mean to them.

WHAT WOULD YOU TOLERATE OR ALLOW?

Not only do we need to be clear about what we mean, but also about what we will tolerate and what level of flexibility we can build into this. Some people believe that a one-night stand is OK, for instance, but that to carry on seeing the person isn't acceptable.

We may need to negotiate or we may agree. We might even decide to leave the relationship altogether. But we need to be very sure that what we decide is what we really want and not what other people have told us we should want.

ED AND SYLVIE'S STORY:
An Agreement

Ed and Sylvie are a middle-class professional couple. They have been married for 20 years. At the outset, they were both very clear that they wanted an open relationship. Ed has been seeing another woman for 10 years and Sylvie has had a lesbian relationship for about the same time. Once a year they all go on holiday together with their various children. This has not been easy all the time, but it works. Ed and Sylvie love each other and have many, many things in common.

Some people are so tolerant that they are happy for their partner to see other people. It might be the very glue that holds their marriage together.

Personally, I think the value of prostitution is underestimated and many men who visit prostitutes can maintain a happy marriage because of it rather than in spite of it.

And sometimes infidelity hurts, but love is stronger than the pain.

VIVIENNE'S STORY:
Another Agreement

Vivienne married at 17. Her husband was abroad constantly and worked in a very glamorous business. She discovered he was having multiple affairs. When she confronted him with it, he said he wasn't prepared to stop but he would not do it at home. Vivienne agreed to this. She thought he was a fantastic person, a great friend, a super father and she loved him. She brought up their children and created a spectacularly successful career for herself. She was very fulfilled.

Now when I visit them I see a very happy relationship. He's stopped having affairs, they have grandchildren and they have a great family life together. It has worked out for Vivienne, but she has had to confront many demons and do a lot of work on herself along the way.

TO TELL OR NOT TO TELL

Do you believe that if you stray you should automatically tell your partner? Have you ever thought that you may be confessing not because you want to be honest but because you'll feel less guilty? Before rushing to tell a partner about a one-night stand, think very carefully about what this might do to your relationship. You might gain more from examining what made you do it in the first place and working on what you really want.

Many people who have affairs are not natural philanderers. A one-night stand might be a childish inability to resist the cookie jar when it's offered, but an ongoing affair is often a sign of dissatisfaction in some area of the relationship.

Whilst it might be useful just to forget the folly of a one-off slip, sometimes an affair brought into the open can start a more honest communication that can move the relationship to another level. But don't make confessions simply to test another's love, patience or tolerance.

LINDA'S STORY:
A Cry for Help

When Linda confessed to her workaholic husband that she'd been having an affair for two years and wanted to leave him for her lover, it prompted the first in-depth talk they'd had for years. They got some help and remembered what they loved about each other. Finally, they decided to give it another go and resolved to talk regularly about their relationship. Linda's affair was a cry for help.

The questions in the relationship survey at the back of this book may help you explore your attitudes to monogamy and fidelity.

FREEDOM OR BALL AND CHAIN?

Two of the questions I asked in my internet relationship survey were:

What do you like about being single?
What do you like about being in a relationship?

About 90 per cent of the people who replied said that the one thing they liked about being single was freedom – 'not having to ask anyone's permission', 'not having to worry about anyone else', 'not being held back by someone else' and 'being able to do what I want, when I want and with whom I want'.

What people liked about being in a relationship was having someone to share things with and be close to, having regular sex and making plans together.

What amazed me was that most of them believed it was impossible to have all these things. I'm suggesting that maybe you *can* have your freedom, do a lot of what you want *and* have all the benefits of having a special person in your life.

What if you set someone free to be who they are, accept that they may have to change paths and feel OK about what happens? The old story about opening the cage and setting the bird free is a simple lesson that many of us aren't paying attention to.

When we approach relationships from a sense of security, we don't feel the need to tie anyone down. And when we let someone be themselves, they may begin to appreciate the way we understand them and may commit to us without even realizing they are committing.

JOSEPHA'S STORY:
A Singular Marriage

Josepha, who has been married for 15 years, told me that she is a commitment phobic. Even when she was waiting to sign the marriage register, she was saying to herself, 'Will I find some reason not to do this?' Yet she has never been unfaithful to her husband and is totally committed to their marriage in spite of the fact that she had a long history of infidelities in previous relationships. She says that despite being married, she still feels as if she's a single woman. Josepha and her husband are one of the most solid and harmonious couples I know.

VALUES

We all have things that are important to us. To a very religious person it might be very important that they marry into their faith. To someone who has been left many times it might be very important to know that their next partner is prepared to stay the course. It might be important that someone is of equal intelligence or wants to live in the sun, or is self-sufficient or independent. Everyone values different things.

If you are a dedicated animal rights activist, it might be very hard to form a relationship with someone who works in a slaughterhouse. If monogamy is important to you, then it's probably a good idea to find someone who thinks the same way. If you are very spontaneous and make last-minute decisions, it might be challenging to be with someone who has to plan everything to the last detail ...

I know a lot of couples who are very happy. When I asked them what were the foundations of that happiness they had a lot of individual reasons. But the one they all had in common was shared values. They believed in the same things.

SARAH AND CRAIG'S STORY:
Mixed Values

Sarah and Craig's eyes locked across a crowded hotel lobby. They spent a very passionate night fuelled by red wine and lust, but it didn't stop there.

Craig worked abroad and Sarah had a busy life as a business consultant. They kept in touch via e-mail and phone calls. Craig asked Sarah to visit him in Zimbabwe and meet his kids. Both of them thought they had found 'that special person'.

When Sarah arrived she found a very different person from that wild spontaneous lover who had first enticed her. When Craig had a crisis at work which took up most of his time Sarah found people to lunch with and was quite content. But Craig felt guilty because he felt he had to be responsible for everyone and when he couldn't, he blamed them.

One evening Sarah made a move to initiate sex. Craig got annoyed. He felt pressurized because in his view men initiated and when he wasn't in charge, he felt insecure and angry.

When Sarah came to see me she was down about the way the relationship was going. Nevertheless she was planning to go back and give it a second go.

I sensed they had a case of clashing values. Both of them had been living a story in their heads that wasn't based on the full facts. And both of them had been so blinded by lust that they hadn't paid attention to what the other had been telling them.

I suggested Sarah work out her values. She'd had a good marriage to her late husband so we started with what she liked about that relationship:

💜 He was intelligent and well-read and loved to socialize, as did Sarah.
💜 He was successful and self-assured.
💜 He had a sense of humour about himself.
💜 He was romantic ...

The list was long, so I asked Sarah to prioritize what was most important. Instantly she said, 'He loved my spontaneity.' Did Craig measure up to that? Sarah replied forcefully, '*No way*. He has to plan everything.'

As we went through the list Sarah realized that Craig didn't read books and was really looking for a corporate wife and a mother for his young kids. Sarah was a well-read intellectual woman who had already done the corporate wife thing and had two grown-up daughters. She was in the process of reinventing and unleashing her sexy self on the world. And the last thing she wanted was more kids.

Sarah had never taken the time to consider in the cold light of day what was important to her in a relationship. When she removed herself from the lust she felt for Craig, she realized this relationship was not for her.

Some of our values are so important that if they aren't honoured, we can't have a relationship at all. And some of them are important, but we're prepared to be flexible and agree to differ. One thing's for sure: it's vital to know what's most important to you.

What are your Relationship Values?

If you are already in a relationship or want to find one that honours your deepest values, you have to clarify what they are.

💜 Take a pen and paper and write a list of what you value in a relationship. Take some time over this, but don't try too hard to think of what you want, just allow the ideas to come up and write them down without editing.

- When you've finished the list, go through each item in turn and notice the feelings you get.
- Decide which of these values is vital to a relationship.
- Next, decide on which ones you think are important but not utterly vital.
- Any that are left are probably those things which would be lovely to have but without which you could still have a pretty decent relationship.

What we usually end up with after this exploration is a bunch of concepts. And you can rest assured that words like 'commitment', 'love' and 'relationship' mean different things to different people. For you, showing commitment might mean only sleeping with one person and for your partner it might mean marriage.

If you have put down words like this, take some time to write out what they mean to you. And if you're doing this exploration with a partner, make sure you understand what they mean by these words. You can explore this further in the relationship survey in the back of this book.

CREATE YOUR OWN MOVIE

'When we are motivated by goals that have deep meaning, by dreams that need completion, by pure love that needs expressing, then we truly live life.'
Greg Anderson

I've met a lot of people who have successful fulfilling relationships and most of them had vivid visions of the life they wanted *and* they believed it would come to them.

TONY'S STORY:
A Fantasy Movie

Three years ago Tony was divorced, living in London and on his own. Now Tony and Alison run a business taking people on sailing trips around the Indian Ocean.

Tony told me that he used to spend a lot of time thinking about his dream life. He said it was like directing a fantasy movie. He'd write the scripts and choose the actors and the locations. He imagined that he would meet a woman who would share his dream of living on the ocean. He didn't plan every move, he just visualized how he wanted it to be and said to himself, 'This is the life that I am going to step into very soon.'

This next exploration is designed to help you create the life you want and manifest it naturally, without relentlessly focusing on your goal to the exclusion of everything else.

Write, Direct and Star in your own Movie

Make sure you have interruption-free time to do this.

Simply imagine you're directing a movie in which you are the star. Like all good directors, you must be prepared to adapt the storylines, change the scripts and the actors and shoot several different endings.

Here are some clues to get you started:

- *Location*: Where is the movie set? You can have lots of different locations if you want. Which country/countries would you be in? Where would you be – countryside, seaside, city, desert? Be as detailed as you want.
- *Wardrobe and make up*: Who would be wearing what? What would you be wearing? How would you look? (Be realistic unless you're thinking plastic surgery!)
- *Scenes*: How does the action begin and what scenes are you going to include?
- *Co-actors*: Who is with you? You might not have a particular person in mind to co-star with you, so make up an idea of someone then look for the star!
- *Action*: How do you interact with this person in the movie? What are you doing together, saying to each other, not doing together? What sort of people do you meet? What adventures are you having? Is this movie *sexy*?
- *Effects*: Make sure you have sound effects, Technicolor and widescreen.
- *Endings*: Write three different happy endings to this movie!

Stepping into your Movie

As you know, when you are seeing a movie as if it's happening to you it's much more powerful emotionally than if it's projected onto a distant screen. To make your movie more real you have to step into it and be part of it.

- ♥ Start to run your movie in your head. Notice where the image is and imagine it coming closer and closer until you meet it and step into it. Feel the difference.
- ♥ Now stand or sit in a way that you feel powerful. Breathe into your sacral area and relax.
- ♥ Let the movie run slowly. Act it out in your head ... and keep doing this as often as you wish. The more you do it, the more it gets into your muscles and the more real it seems. If you believe in it and really feel it in your body, then it's much more likely to come true.
- ♥ Now that you've seen the movie, put it away and allow it to roll out in its own good time.

Energy follows thought. What you think you are is what you become.

CONNECTING

John Donne, the metaphysical poet, said that no man is an island unto himself. That's one of the truest things I know. Unless you're living like a hermit, you're going to be constantly meeting new people. Being able to connect with them in a special way can make the difference between finding love or letting it pass you by. Whether you are single or in a relationship, this section has some valuable people-connecting tools that you can use in any area of your life.

If you've read this far, congratulations. Chances are you've got to know and love yourself more and you are aware of how wonderful you are. Armed with a sense of how you want your life to be and a heart that's open, you are more than ready to give your friendship and love. You know where you stand on certain topics and you've developed a sense of the kind of relationships and people that you are going to attract. And of course, you *are* going to attract them.

So what happens when you meet someone for the first time?

THE FIRST ENCOUNTER

A date is simply an appointment to meet someone and beyond that it is an opportunity to explore that person *and* yourself.

You know that feeling before you go for a job interview? You have to sell yourself in a short period of time and you know you won't get another chance. I've been for some job interviews where I've known that it was exactly what I wanted. And I've been for others where I've thought, 'Oh well, it's a job and I can do it.' And I've been for others where I thought it was what I wanted but discovered it wasn't!

Some of us go into an interview thinking that the decision is entirely that of the interviewer. We ask ourselves anxiously, 'Will they pick me?' Some of us go in with the attitude that they will be bowled over by our skills. We say to ourselves, 'How can they resist me?' And some clever people go into an interview knowing what they want and being open to finding out if what they are offering is right for the job and, even more importantly, if the job is offering them what they want. They say to themselves, 'Whatever happens, it's going to be interesting.'

A date is very much like a job interview – first impressions count and the first encounter determines whether there'll be a second. The difference is that you don't have to make any quick life-changing decisions when you are dating. It can go on as long as you need to discover whether to move to the next level or say 'Ciao, it's been fun!'

THE EIGHT KEYS TO INTUITIVE DATING

'There isn't any formula for loving. You learn to love … by paying attention and doing what one thereby discovers has to be done.'

Aldous Huxley

1. Remember that there are two people on the date and each of you has your own unique agenda of expectations, dreams, beliefs and rules.
2. Be curious and open to finding out more about the person. Imagine you are about to open a mystery present.
3. Be playful. If you have a sense of fun and transmit that to another person, they're much more likely to join in.
4. Be prepared to ask questions before judging them.
5. Listen to your intuition and pay attention to 'trigger' feelings and what causes them.

6. Remember you are always learning something about yourself when you interact with other people.

7. Be OK with whatever happens. Even if it doesn't work out, it'll be a good story to tell your friends.

8. Be yourself. You don't want anyone to fall in love with someone you're not!

REVIEWING

After an encounter with a new person it can be quite useful to review your impressions and clarify your feelings. The next exploration will give you some ideas.

Reviewing an Encounter

Your Impressions

- What was your first impression and your last one? If it changed, what happened?
- Do you like this person?
- Can you talk to them?
- Are you attracted to them?
- What do you like about them?
- What don't you like?
- What emotions do you feel when you think about the likes and dislikes?
- If you were on a date, were you making decisions very early on? What were they based on?
- What do you want to happen next?
- How can you make it happen?
- What rules might be stopping you?
- What else might stop it from happening?
- During the encounter, what did you learn about yourself?

Assumptions and Judgements

When you're answering these questions, be wary of any assumptions you might be making.

- Have you judged the person in any way?
- What evidence do you have? Is it enough to convict them?
- Do they deserve another chance?
- What have you assumed from their words and actions or lack of words or actions?
- On what evidence do you base these assumptions?

It might be useful to remember 'innocent until proven guilty'. Sometimes we can be very hasty. But if you are worried about something, follow it up, find out more.

What Did You Reveal about Yourself?

Just check yourself from time to time as well and recognize what you do. Awareness of a problem is halfway to a solution.

- What roles might you have been playing? Were you repeating any of your patterns?
- How open and honest were you being? Give yourself marks out of 10, with 10 being where you were totally yourself and 1 where you were putting on a big act.
- Did you play any games? Some people pretend they are really interested in something when they're not, or they pretend that something doesn't bother them when it does.
- What did you give away about yourself?
- Is there anything you regret revealing? What do you fear as a result of revealing something?
- What were you holding back?
- Did you get a sense of wanting to reveal something more? If so, what?
- What would you like to reveal next time?
- Was there something you wanted to ask but didn't?

LOVE AT SECOND SIGHT?

There's such a 'romantic' attachment to the idea of love at first sight, but instant attraction isn't always the key to lasting love. Love can and does happen at second, third and even tenth sight, and sometimes years after first sight.

ALAN AND SAMANTHA'S STORY:
Two Bites at the Cherry

Alan and Samantha met at school. They got on well and liked each other a lot but they were just friends. Sam always had the hots for Alan, but he wasn't that interested in her. Both went on to college and married different people.

When they met each other again 34 years later via a schools reunion website, they were both single. Sam told Alan how she'd always had a soft spot in her heart for him. Alan realized that Sam had grown into a beautiful woman who was not just a nice girl but someone he really fancied. Now they're a couple. It took time, but they got there in the end!

So before you discard a parcel because you don't like the wrapping, why not check out what's inside? After all, sometimes the plainest of packages contains the most beautiful prizes and sometimes the most beautiful packages don't always contain the best prizes!

A SPECIAL WORD ABOUT INTERNET DATING

As I write this a friend of mine is flying to California to meet a man she hooked up with online. She's single, bright, attractive, self-sufficient and reasonably sane! Level-headed as she is, I wasn't surprised when she asked me, 'Is it possible to fall in love on the internet?'

Let's consider the process of internet dating.

First, the fact that someone is displaying themselves in this medium suggests that a) they're available and b) they're looking for love. We don't have to go through the 'I fancy them but are they already with someone?' stage because we have that information already. (I know that some people go onto these sites and pretend to be single when they're not, but that happens in real life too. Remember, it's a lot easier to find out about someone by e-mail first before committing to several dates to get the same information!)

Generally the first thing we do is check whether a person's photograph fits our physical template. If it appears to do so we eagerly move on to read their profile. When we discover that they appear to have similar values and a lifestyle that could blend with ours, we get even more excited. We're building up feelings before we've even met them!

Then we start e-mailing. E-mailing is a high-tech version of old fashioned love letters. And it's easy to send several e-mails a day and get excited about the frequent contact. We can go from friendly through subtle to flirtatious and end up being plain raunchy and all in a very short space of time. Somehow it seems easier to let it all hang out when we're hiding behind a computer screen.

We don't even have to be in someone's presence to generate lust. We can be attracted by their openness and manner of expression and the things we have in common and we start to think sexy and before we know it we're lusting after them. But it's important to remember that you are generating this *yourself*. You won't know if there is a sexual spark between you until you meet in the flesh.

And all this time we haven't yet experienced our internet contact's ongoing everyday behaviour. We haven't done the day-to-day things with them. We've not even had to agree where or when to meet or what we're going to do, because the internet is time and activity unspecific. You can connect at 3 a.m. or 3 p.m. and they'll pick it up when it's convenient. And to cap it all, we don't have access to their body language and they can't see if we're shy or fluffing our words. One friend of mine says it takes him an hour to compose an e-mail because he checks it over so many times, rewriting it until it's 'right'. Virtual encounters are very, very different from reality and much easier. So many of the normal dating obstacles have been removed. And without even meeting someone, we're hooked. We're 'in love'.

However, I don't think you can fall truly in love until you've met someone in person and spent enough time with them to really get to know them. If you are looking to make a commitment, I'd think that was quite important, wouldn't you? And I do think it takes time.

Of course, if you want to develop a long-distance relationship, or even a cyber-sex relationship or a friendship or whatever kind of relationship you want, the internet is a great way of kicking it off ... And sooner or later you're going to want to meet that person.

MORE REVIEWING

When we like someone and we are interested in them, it's natural that we'll go home after a date and think about the time we've spent with them. Sometimes we'll talk to our friends and analyse what's going on. Sometimes we'll write things down in a diary. And sometimes we'll just let it all go round and round in our head. And it can get muddled up or polluted by well-meaning friends giving their opinions on a situation they've not even experienced! Some things can become more important than they need to be and we might miss out on others.

Keeping a file or making a map about what's going on will help you clarify your thoughts. Here are some pointers. Feel free to add in your own ideas.

Reviewing a Person

After you've been on a date with someone or just met someone new for the first time, sit down, take a few breaths and relax. Then consider the following questions:

- **How did they behave?**
    What did they do that you liked/disliked and why?
    What did they say that you liked/disliked and why?
    What words do they use frequently?
    Are they always on the go or more laid back?
- **What are they good at and what skills do they have?**
    What do they enjoy doing?
    Are they good with people, things or information?
    What kind of work do they do?
- **What drives them and what's important to them?**
    What clues did they give away as to their political or religious leanings?
    What did they tell you about what they want?
    Do they like their work?
        If they do, what do they like about it?
        If they don't, what would they rather be doing?
    What's important to them?
    What are they looking for?

💜 **Who do they think they are?**

How do they define themselves? (Some people are their work, others their families, others their class – and some, of course, are just themselves.)

It might also help to think about these questions before you meet them again so that you can find out more about who they are and how they live their life.

LEARNING THEIR ENERGETIC LANGUAGE

Look around at people. They have different ways of moving around, don't they? Some of them can't sit still they're so wired and some of them are really chilled and laid back and some are inbetweenies. Ways of moving range from slow and solid to jumpy and light or fast and fiery, and some people have that sexy hip sway ...

This is the language of our bodies. We're not talking 'folded arms means resistance' or 'looking away means rejection' body language, but the overall language of movement and how it varies from person to person. I call it our 'energetic language'.

Sometimes we get irritated or disturbed by different people's energy. If you are really chilled lounging in your chair looking at the clouds and someone keeps chattering fast and furiously, it can be disturbing. If you are walking fast down the street, it can be disturbing to be with someone who just ambles along.

If you are like me, you may not have thought seriously about what kind of energy you are putting out to people. I used to rush in to hug people and some of them would pull back and I'd judge them because they weren't like me.

The cool thing is that when you know what someone's energetic language is, you can be flexible and raise or lower your energy level a little to open out the channels of communication. If you are a slow speaker, wouldn't you be more interested in listening if someone slowed down to your pace? Of course you would.

Another cool thing is that once you become aware of your energy style, you may discover that you do too much of some things and not enough of others. Being aware can help you to become more balanced.

All this helped me make sense of some of the reactions I got from other people. It helped me become very sensitive to people of different energy levels and very flexible.

We all have a preferred energy style, but taking on other styles can be very beneficial. It's like being a chameleon. We can change and shift and still be who we are.

My boyfriend feels that if he's doing any exercise-related activity he has to pump the heart and build up the aerobics. I like to bimble around a park slowly, just experiencing the trees and the deer and smelling stuff. As you can imagine, our cycling energy styles are very different! But when we take on the other's style from time to time, we both benefit. I get some good aerobic exercise and he gets to chill out.

IT'S ELEMENTAL

It's useful to think of energy styles as being like the elements, because fire, air, water and earth all have distinct associations which are very similar to the different energy styles people exhibit. Here are some clues to watch out for.

Fast Burning

They're always bobbing around, appear very busy and might be waving their hands around a lot in fast jabbing movements.

They walk as if they are being led by their head and neck.

They may talk very rapidly and loudly.

Sometimes when you are around them you feel exhausted and sometimes you are warmed and enthused by their powerful energy.

Airy Fairy

They may be waving their arms around a lot, sometimes haphazardly.

They may walk in light but not always rhythmical ways.

They are to be heard talking both quickly and slowly.

Sometimes you don't know where you are with them because they're all over the place and sometimes you rise up on their current and fly.

Liquid Flow

They probably move in a quite rhythmical manner.

They may sashay along in a hip-swinging sexy way.

Their speech might be a little slow but will often have a rhythmical flow.

Sometimes they seem to wash right over you and it can be overwhelming and sometimes you can feel as though you are just floating along.

Solid as a Rock

They probably move quite deliberately and slowly.

They have a heavy and sometimes plodding walk.

They talk slowly and deliberately.

Sometimes being with them can be very tiring and sometimes it can be very relaxing and grounding and calming.

Don't just take my word for this. Go out and experiment. Start watching people and noticing the different styles.

Looking at Styles

When you have worked out your own style, look at the people you feel comfortable with most of the time.

- What kind of style do they have?
- Is it similar to yours?
- Is it very different?
- What do you gain from being around this person?
- What style might it be useful for you to adopt more often and how would that help you?

In the next chapter you'll be learning how to take on different energy styles and use them as a tool for communicating more effectively.

LEARNING THEIR VERBAL LANGUAGE

The words and phrases people use are good clues to how they operate and how they sense the world. This information can come in very useful when communicating with people, as you'll find out in the next chapter. For now, just start to be aware of the different styles.

SEE, FEEL, HEAR

Most people have a preferred way of sensing the world and other people. This doesn't mean that they don't use their other senses. They do. It's just that when they describe what they sense to themselves they tend to prefer a certain mode. Some people pick up on the visual aspects. Others are highly tuned to what they hear. And others get more of a feel for things. The words they use are clues as to what's their preferred sense. And they find it easier to understand someone who is also 'talking their language'.

As you listen to someone talk, notice which kind of words they use most – 'seeing' words, 'hearing' words or 'feeling' words. Try it on yourself first.

Your Way of Sensing

* Write out a description of a place or activity or something that you can remember in detail.
* How did you describe it?
* When you think about it now, what are you doing? Are you remembering more sounds, sights or feelings?
* Write out another description of the same place or activity and try to include sensory descriptions that you didn't use in the last piece you wrote. If you realized you wrote mostly in feeling words, try using more visual words. If you talked about how the place sounded, concentrate on what it looked like too.

HOW DO THEY OPERATE?

We all have different strategies for doing things. Being aware of someone's strategies means that you are prepared for how they might react to things and you will understand why they react the way they do. It also means that you can use their strategies to communicate more harmoniously. We'll be looking at communicating in the next section. Meanwhile, here are some ways of behaving that you might pick up on.

'I WANT' OR 'I DON'T WANT'

People are motivated to do things for very different reasons. Knowing their motivation can be very useful when you are trying to persuade them to do something or to communicate more effectively. Knowing your own style can be useful too!

Most of us act from one of two motives: we want to get away from something we don't like or we want to move towards something we do like.

For example, a smoker might be motivated to stop smoking because they are terrified of dying of a smoking-related disease. This is what we call an 'away-from' strategy. Or they might be motivated to stop because they want to be able to run fast or live longer. This would be a 'towards' strategy.

Here's some clues to look out for.

- 'I don't want'
  They tell you what they don't want.
  They are kicked into action by pressure or deadlines.
  They will notice the flaws in a plan or focus on what might go wrong. (This might make them sound negative, but it can be essential.)
  They love having a problem to solve.
  They respond well to fear of what might happen if they don't do something.
- 'I want'
  They are motivated by achieving and the thought of success.
  They have things they work towards, whether it's winning an award or building a house or getting a date.
  They tend to ignore or play down problems.
  They respond well to temptation.

Be careful of judging one way or other as better. They are just different. And being aware of them can help you understand yourself and someone else more clearly.

If you gave my boyfriend and me the same book to read we would approach it very differently. I would take the book, skim the contents and open it. I might look at the front first or I might just flick through it. If I found something that interested me in the middle of the book, I'd start to read it. If you asked me what was in the book, I'd probably be able to give you an overall sense but I'd most likely not be aware of many specifics.

He, on the other hand, would begin at the beginning. He'd probably read the back cover and he'd have his yellow highlighter pen ready. He'd notice every typo and spot linguistic and logical inaccuracies. He'd read the book slowly, moving through it in an orderly fashion. If you asked him what was in it, chances are he'd be able to describe things in great detail.

I pay attention to the big picture and he pays attention to detail.

Most of us have a tendency one way or another and of course balance is about being able to see the big picture *and* be aware of useful details.

People's strategies affect how they make decisions and how they like to take in information. Knowing which preference someone has can be very useful when you want to communicate something important to them or cajole them into doing something that they might enjoy. Knowing your own strategy can also help you understand why you find some people so strange. So, instead of judging them, maybe it's time to just acknowledge the difference and celebrate it.

What strategies do you use in making decisions and in taking in information?

WHERE ARE THEY COMING FROM?

When I was younger we used to say to people: 'Where are you coming from?' What we meant was: 'What's behind what you're doing? What's driving you?'

From time to time we all tend to take different stances on subjects. Sometimes we have set ways of looking at things that aren't always useful. But when you pay attention to someone, you can begin to decipher where they're coming from.

NIALL'S STORY:
'That's How It's Always Been'

Niall never expected any relationship to go past the nine-month mark because he'd had two relationships which had ended after six to eight months.

Niall is coming from a 'That's how it's always been' position that *expects history to repeat itself.*

LOUISE'S STORY:
'Why Change?'

Louise was perfectly happy in her relationship with Chris. She saw him at weekends and on Wednesday evenings. Chris suggested that sometimes they might want to see each other on different nights. Louise couldn't understand.

Louise is coming from a 'Why change?' position where she sees things as *remaining the same.*

OLIVIA'S STORY:
'It's Impossible'

Olivia wanted to be a dancer. She'd done some lessons but had settled down to a regular job. She said, 'I've got as much chance of becoming a dancer as my cat has of learning to eat with a knife and fork.'

Olivia is coming from an 'It's impossible' position where her dreams will *never come true*, for example 'What's the point of asking? They'll never say yes.'

It's interesting to be aware of where you are coming from and notice if it is ever any of the above positions. Perhaps you come from the opposite positions. Check out people you meet. They'll give away clues as to where they are coming from. People-detecting skills are easy to develop if you pay attention and it can be great fun putting them into action.

Again, this will all help you understand why people do what they do and enable you to be more flexible in your dealings with them.

LEARN FROM THEIR STORIES

We all tell each other stories. Storytelling is a social activity and a way of telling people about ourselves. The stories people tell about their past relationships, how they are at work and how they treat their friends are superb clues to their personality.

HOW THEY BEHAVED

Pay special attention to how someone has treated people in previous relationships. If it is consistent, the chances are that in similar circumstances they're going to behave in the same way to you.

IRENE AND KEVIN'S STORY:
'Over Attentiveness'

Irene started a relationship with Kevin, who was married. After some time they realized they wanted to be together. Kevin was very careful not to make matters worse for his wife. Although he wanted to leave her because they had grown apart and Irene was so much more in tune with him, he didn't want to hurt her. He was even thinking about letting her have a bigger share of their property. Irene came to me because she was very concerned about what she saw as Kevin's 'over attentiveness' to his wife.

I asked her if she could see that Kevin's attentiveness to his wife showed that he was a kind and fair person. I asked her to imagine for a moment that she and Kevin were separating. Would she want him to be bitter and greedy with her and treat her coldly? Something clicked.

KIM AND NIGEL'S STORY:
No. 1

When Kim started going out with Nigel she thought he was her dream man. He was charming, intelligent, rich, great fun and he made her feel very special. One day Nigel was telling her about his father and his mistress. 'My grandfather was the same,' he said. 'It seems odd, but the men in my family seem to have a propensity for keeping more than one woman.' Kim wanted to ask if he was like that but she didn't. She put it to the back of her mind.

After about eight months, she found out that not only was he seeing his ex-wife, but also a former girlfriend. When she confronted him with this, he said, 'But you're no.1.' He'd virtually warned her a long time ago, but she hadn't listened. Maybe she hadn't wanted to. Who knows?

I'm not suggesting that you hear stories and make all kinds of assumptions. But listen out for warnings. The more alert you are, the more you're going to pick up on stories like Nigel's. If you hear something like this, be prepared to find out more. And then you can decide what to do.

WHAT'S IMPORTANT TO THEM

Stories are also a great way of picking up on what's really important to someone and learning valuable lessons.

DEREK AND CYNTHIA'S STORY:
Smiling Instead

When Derek met Cynthia they talked a lot about their exes. They were still at the 'complaining' stage. Derek used to complain that his ex always scowled. He used to say, 'She didn't realize how ugly she made herself when she did that.'

Cynthia remembered this and each time she began to make a nasty face at something Derek said, she'd stop herself and smile. This was a very useful lesson. Cynthia didn't want to be a scowler, whether she was with Derek or not. And when I asked Derek what was special about Cynthia, one of the things he mentioned was how her 'happy smiling face' brightened up his day.

PAULA AND TIM'S STORY:
Being Interested

Paula told Tim how she'd left Al because he was always bringing her work down. She writes about health and beauty and Al used to scoff, 'That's not real writing, that's just women's mag stuff.' He never read her work and they rarely discussed it.

Tim remembered this. He wasn't very interested in women's beauty but he decided to find out about what Paula did. He loved seeing her light up when she talked about her work and he would ask questions when he didn't understand. Tim learned from the story of Al and he also learned a lot about women's health and beauty. Paula's friends think Tim is 'so easy to talk to' and Paula is proud of the fact that her husband is a hit with her friends!

By now you may have embarked on the relationship journey. On this voyage of discovery you will be exploring not only someone else, but also yourself. And you want to make it work, don't you?

No matter how madly in love you may be, life will keep on coming at you, and if you're not going to sink in the seas of love you'll need the skills of communicating, creating and maintaining relation-ships. You'll find it even easier to weather the storms and sail into calmer waters after you've read the next chapter ...

CHAPTER 6

COMMUNICATING, CREATING AND BUILDING

COMMUNICATING: THE POWER OF LANGUAGE

'If you aren't communicating who you are in every interaction with others there is nothing separating you from all the noise we are bombarded with every day.'

Kendrick Cleveland

Great communicators make natural use of a variety of language patterns that enhance their interactions with other people. You can learn how to adapt these patterns to enrich your own communications in a way that's naturally right for you.

TALKING TO YOURSELF

How you communicate to yourself directly influences how you communicate to other people. What's your 'self-talk' like?

Most of us spend a lot of time talking to ourselves, either out loud or in our head, and sadly most of what we say is negative. Sometimes the voices are our own and sometimes they are other people's. Either way, these negative voices are very damaging. But it stands to reason that if we are capable of creating voices that rebuke, criticize and demotivate us, we are also capable of creating positive encouraging voices. It just takes a little practice.

JANET'S STORY:
'There's No Way ...'

Janet wanted to take a part-time job, but whenever she thought about discussing it with her husband, she heard herself saying, 'There's no way he'll agree to this,' and she kept quiet.

When I worked with Janet, I got her to create a new voice. She chose to say, 'Robert will be open to anything that makes me happy.' I asked her to make the voice sound sexy and melodious and to make it come from the same direction and appear in the same location as the negative voice.

Getting in Touch with your Voices

What unhelpful messages are you regularly broadcasting to yourself? Take a moment to listen.

- Whose voice is it?
- What direction is it coming from?
- Where can you hear it?
- What does it sound like?
- What specific words are you using?

Work out what you'd like to hear instead of your negative voice and how you'd like to hear it – sexy, soft, teasing, you choose. Then start repeating it over and over. Every time you hear the negative voice, replace it with the new voice.

Many of my clients have enjoyed playing their favourite motivating tune in their heads as a prelude to creating the positive voice. If you have music that 'sends' you, play it in your head, turn up the volume and use it to blast out your negative voices.

Keep doing this until the old tape wears out and the new one is built in.

THE ART OF QUESTIONING

When talking to someone else, especially for the first time, so many of my clients worry about what they're going to say. I encourage them instead to focus on finding out about the other person. Questions were designed for this purpose. Questioning skills are equally valuable when engaging in an important discussion with a loved one.

The question you ask will directly influence the quality and type of answer you get. Good questions get the information you want, clarify what someone means and help you to understand what makes them tick. Bad questions can get someone so irritated that you sabotage the purpose of the communication.

QUESTION FOREPLAY

Sometimes just asking a question directly can be a little harsh. That's why good communicators use what I call 'question foreplay'.

These phrases are a gentle way of leading into asking a question:

'I'm curious to know whether ...'
'Would you share with me ...?'
'I'd appreciate your telling me ...'
'I wonder whether ...'
'I hope you won't mind telling me ...'

The following phrases give the impression that you're asking permission to ask a question and put people at their ease:

'I wonder if you'd mind me asking ...?'
'Can I ask you a question ...?'

'Would it be OK for me to ask you ...?'

'I'd like to ask you a bit more about ...'

'There's something I want to clarify, so would you be able to answer a couple of questions?'

OPEN OR CLOSED

The type of question you ask will also determine the type of response you get. Questions generally fall into two categories: open and closed.

> Open questions create a sense of possibility and closed questions get specific information.
>
> Open questions create rapport and encourage someone to share their thoughts with you.
>
> Closed questions are great for asking for agreement and clarifying what someone means.

Here are some variations on open and closed questions and the types of answers they encourage:

Closed: 'Can we go away next weekend?' Purpose: You want agreement and you're asking for a simple answer.

Closed confirming: 'So, let me clarify. Are you saying that you'd like to go away next weekend but you may have to work and you'll know by Thursday?' Purpose: You want to check that you understand what they mean.

Closed limiting: 'Do you want to make love now or later?' Purpose: To let the person know you expect to make love and to find out when they want to do it, not if!

Open facilitating: 'What did you like about the best holiday you've ever had?' Purpose: You want to know about the person and are willing to let them express themselves fully.

Open direct: 'What do you want?' 'What do you need me to do?' 'How can I help?' 'What would you like to do this weekend?' Purpose: You want to know the other person's thoughts and are willing to let them express themselves fully.

Open sharing: 'How can we spend more time together and keep our independence?' Purpose: To create an idea of joint responsibility and a willingness to listen to the other person's ideas with a sense that you will contribute afterwards.

LEADING QUESTIONS

You can also use questions to lead someone towards a specific answer. These questions can be great for getting people to think in different ways but they can also be manipulative. Knowing how this works will help you recognize when people are trying to manipulate you.

Some questions say strongly: 'This is what I think and I'm assuming you agree with me.' Take, for example, 'You do want to have children, don't you?' or 'You aren't planning to move in with me, are you?'

The danger here is that someone may feel intimidated and just go along with you even if it's not really what they want. That could lead to big problems.

Some questions make assumptions and also seem to fence people in, for example: 'What shall we eat tonight, Thai or Mexican?' This question assumes you do want to eat out tonight, you are eating together and that the choice is only Thai or Mexican. When you're working with an indecisive person, this could be useful, but it can also be very manipulative.

You can still lead people by asking gently suggestive questions, for example: 'I'd love to eat out tonight and quite fancy Thai or Mexican. How about you?' This question puts your point of view, but also offers them a chance to voice theirs.

THE DANGERS OF 'WHY?'

It's our nature to want to know why things happen, but asking why isn't always useful. It can elicit a stream of answers that we don't want to hear or that don't help the situation. To take a couple of examples:

💜   Your partner says, 'I feel used by you.'

Here, if you ask why, the chances are they'll come up with a list of complaints about you. What if you were to ask instead:

'How did you come to that conclusion?'

'What makes you think that I am using you?'

'In what way do you feel used?'

'If this is the case, what would you like me to do differently?'

Here you are asking them for evidence, making them take responsibility for their feelings and also asking, 'What do you want instead?' This makes them think about the possibilities of what could be rather than wallow in what is.

♥ Your partner says, 'I want you to be more romantic.'

Here they obviously have a standard for 'romantic' and believe that you are in some way not living up to it. It might be useful to find out what that standard is. So, instead of rushing off to the florist's for a dozen roses, you might ask:

'What does "romantic" mean to you?'

'More romantic than what?'

'What would I have to do to be romantic enough for you?'

Maybe you can do it, maybe you can't, but at least you'll have a good idea of what they're expecting or wanting!

Each time you find yourself wanting to ask your loved one 'Why?', stop and ask yourself: 'How else could I phrase this?'

HONEST LANGUAGE
ABSOLUTELY ALWAYS NEVER

Have you ever used the words 'always', 'never' and 'everyone' in an untruthful way? I certainly have. 'You always tell me off when I leave the bottle tops off.' 'You never bring me flowers.' What we really mean is: 'You don't do this very often' or 'You tend to do this quite frequently.' And when someone hears 'always' and 'never', they immediately feel accused of a crime they didn't commit. No wonder people get cross with us.

Kiss, Kiss

Pam liked her lover to kiss her hello. Sometimes he walked in and started talking before kissing her. Once she confronted him and said, 'You *never* kiss me when we meet!'

What Pam said didn't get her what she wanted. She wanted him to kiss her more often and she should have said just that: 'I want you to kiss me more.'

Her lover might have answered, 'Don't you remember how I kissed you hello yesterday when we met up outside the restaurant?' and she might have replied, 'That's true and I appreciate it and I'd like you to do more of that because it makes me feel warm towards you!'

Instead her attacking attitude was likely to produce a defensive response.

If someone uses these words with you, you can gently remind them of what they're doing and attempt to tease out what they really mean.

Be very wary of using this type of language yourself.

ARE YOU A MIND READER?

There is nothing more annoying than someone accusing you of having hidden motives or assuming they know what you think. Yet most of us indulge in the game of mind-reading on a regular basis, saying things like:

'You did that to annoy me.'

'You don't want to come running with me because I'm too slow.'

'I bet you're wishing I'd shut up.'

'You'd love this, it's just up your street.'

Over the years, you and I have learned verbal behaviour we didn't ask to learn. We know very well how to fantasize, fabricate, judge, assume and draw conclusions without much evidence.

Sometimes we intuitively know what's going on with someone, but sometimes we're way off mark.

How about saying instead:

'I don't know what drove you to do this, but I'm annoyed.'

'I was wondering if there was a reason why you don't want to come running with me?'

'Am I talking too much or are you just a good listener?'

'You might like to take a look at this. Let me know what you think.'

When we take responsibility for our own emotions and suggest rather than give orders, our communication will be much more relaxed, open and welcome.

TALKING THEIR LANGUAGE
SIGHTS, SOUNDS AND FEELINGS

In the last chapter I introduced you to the idea that people use different sensory words to make sense of the world. You can make use of their preferences to create fantastic rapport in your communication.

If you were going to suggest eating in a certain place or going somewhere on holiday, wouldn't it make sense to describe it in the mode that appeals to the other person?

- Zak uses lots of touchy-feely words and talks about getting to grips with things or how he likes the feel of a place or the vibes someone gives off. If I wanted him to come to my favourite restaurant, I'd give him a feel for the warm atmosphere and the way you sink into the floor cushions and the different textures of the food.
- Tina's a very visually-oriented person. She often talks about getting clarity and enthuses about the quality of light reflected on things. Her sense of colour and ability to blend shades is second to none. If I wanted Tina to come with me I'd get her to visualize the rich burgundy cushions with gold thread and I'd describe the beauty of the food's presentation using colour and contrast.
- Jack's very sound oriented. When he described a tour he'd done of the jungle he went on about the sounds. He often says things like 'That really resonates with me.' If I wanted to get Jack to this restaurant, I'd sound off about the music they play and how you can talk without being overheard whilst still being aware of the gentle buzz of conversation. I might even tell him about the sizzle of the prawns they cook at the table or the crusty sound of fresh bread being bitten into.

With a little imagination you can create temptingly descriptive language for all sorts of situations.

Here are some words I like to use depending on the different modes people favour. Come up with some of your own for each category.

Visual words: Shimmering, shining, glowing, crystal clear, myriad of colours, muted tones, light and airy, glowing, translucent

Sound words: Smooth, crisp, crunchy, soft, resonate, tuned in, on the wavelength, harmonious, tinkling

Touchy-feely words: Velvety, smooth, gliding, slippery, soft, juicy, vibes, feel

Tasty words: Delicious, yummy, tasty, scrumptious, lip-lickingly good

A fun way of getting into the swing of this is to find someone who uses a different mode from you and ask them to describe a favourite activity or a place they love to go on holiday. Then you can have fun describing to them a holiday, activity or meal in their mode. Aim to make it as tempting as possible. Notice how they react.

TRIGGER WORDS

One thing that really gets my back up is when someone tells me I *must* do something, even if it's something they've enjoyed. Instead of encouraging me, it makes me want to rebel. Most of us have trigger words that send us into 'You're bossing me around' mode.

Here are some common trigger words that get people going:

must

should

ought to

have to

want to

need to

These trigger words will commonly generate one of two distinct feelings for most people, either 'I'm not doing *that*' or 'I'm up for *that!*'

Trying Out Trigger Words

Think of something that is coming up in your life that would have positive effects for you. It could be exercising, going out more or just being more flirtatious. Use different trigger words and notice your feelings as you say them to yourself, for example:

> 'I must be more flirtatious.'
> 'I ought to be more flirtatious.'
> 'I should be more flirtatious.'
> 'I have to be more flirtatious.'
> 'I want to be more flirtatious.'
> 'I could be more flirtatious.'

Which trigger word made you feel more compelled to be more flirtatious?

Next time someone uses one of the motivator words that don't appeal to you, just be aware that your reactions are triggered by the word, let go of the emotion and put in your favourite trigger word. You might feel very different!

Remember that other people are also put off by certain trigger words. A much nicer way to trigger someone's delight is to use less commanding and more suggestive words, for example:

> 'You might enjoy trying that restaurant.'
> 'You may like to try that restaurant.'
> 'I've an idea you'd like that restaurant.'

This way, people feel as if you're respecting their right to choose.

'DESCRIBER' WORDS

There's an old saying: 'When in Rome, do as the Romans do.' As an English person, I talk about 'lifts', 'boots', 'the loo' and 'braces'. When I'm talking to Americans, I substitute their words and talk about 'elevators', 'trunks', 'the bathroom' and 'suspenders'.

We all use our own special words to describe our feelings and reactions. Most of us don't realize that the words that turn us on might not do it for other people.

ANDREW'S STORY:
'Good Effort'

Andrew uses the words 'good effort' when he praises someone for doing something well. He told me that his wife often complained that she never felt fully appreciated by him.

When I asked Andrew to pay attention to how *she* gave out praise he discovered that she is much more effusive. 'Wow, that was fantastic. You did a brilliant job.' The next time Andrew praised his wife he used her words. Her reaction was much more positive.

When someone uses our words, we feel a bond with them. At some unconscious level we're saying to ourselves, 'They're like me.'

The sexual words we use are particularly important to us. People will use different words for a penis or a vagina or various sexual activities. If you can learn to use someone's sexy words, they're going to feel more comfortable with you and possibly a lot more turned on.

Start to notice people's 'describer words' and use them back to them. It will really help develop mutual rapport.

'DOING' THEIR LANGUAGE
FLEXI-STYLES

If you've read the last chapter about different energy styles, you'll realize the value of being able to moderate the level and nature of your energy to make someone feel more comfortable *(see page 115)*.

MAGGIE AND DAVE'S STORY:
'Slow Down!'

In the early days of their relationship when Maggie wanted to tell Dave something exciting, she'd rush in firing on all cylinders and no matter what he was doing she'd burst out with the good news. Dave would move back, put up his hands and shout: 'Slow down!' Maggie would get upset and accuse him of dampening her enthusiasm.

When she realized how different their energies were, she practised stepping into Dave's style before she rushed in. She still kept all the excitement bubbling up inside her, but she walked into the room more slowly, got his attention by tapping him on the shoulder and asked him if he'd got a moment as she had something she really wanted to tell him about.

When she did this as well as slowing down her usual rate of speech and putting the excitement into her voice rather than her movements, Dave responded in a very different way. Maggie wasn't being any less herself, but she was adapting herself to make Dave feel more comfortable and thus get her point across more easily.

Is there anyone who has a very different energy from you and with whom it's important you connect? Try moderating or accelerating your energy to be more like theirs and see what happens.

GESTURES

When people are communicating, they don't just use specific words, they also send out individual and unique signals and gestures.

When you pay attention, you'll notice how people tend to mark out particular locations in the space around them, perhaps by moving their hands or with a tilt of their head or a certain body posture. When they refer to the topic again, it's very likely that they'll use the same gestures in the same locations as well as the same words.

You can use these gestures and words to create a very powerful type of unconscious rapport with people.

When I asked Lorna to tell me about a time she last felt really connected to a man, she lifted her hands with the palms facing her face and wiggled her fingers. She said it was a 'gooey but powerful' feeling.

A bit later in the conversation I reminded her of this by saying, 'Wow, that gooey powerful feeling is really strong for you, isn't it?' in a voice tone and rhythm and intonation that was as close to hers as possible and at the same time I repeated her gestures exactly. She went straight back into the feeling and remarked how I really seemed to understand how she felt!

How can you do this?

- Pay attention to people and be alert for their repetitive signals and gestures.
- Next time you talk to someone, imagine they are surrounded by a globe with horizontal and vertical grid lines and use this as a visual aid to map out the location of their gestures and their glances.
- If you not only remember the words they use but also know where and how they gesture and look when they feel good or when they made a great decision, you can recreate the situation for them.

Being able to piece together the map of how they operate and use what you learn has several benefits. You can recreate specific feelings for them and they will feel that you really understand them. This can make them much more open to your ideas and to seeing your side of a negotiation.

CREATING

CREATIVE CONTRACTS – ME, YOU AND WE

It's amazing how lightly we treat our relationships compared to our jobs. When we go for a job, we make sure that we know the terms and conditions and we agree to abide by those terms. When we go into a relationship, we often have no idea what sort of contract we're entering into.

Some people believe that formal agreements put a damper on love by even suggesting it might end. They prefer to think that if you love someone you'll work it out. Judging by the terrible stories of divorce battles that we hear every day, I'm not so sure this is true.

When the hormonal lust dies down and the rose-coloured glasses come off, life gets real. If you are planning to move in with someone or get married, then it's important to discuss not just your hopes and dreams but also the practical things.

Two friends of mine have been married for 24 years. Six months after they got together they drew up a legal and comprehensive 'relationship contract'. To them the idea of pooling their resources and managing their own planned family and the extended family was too important to leave to chance.

I'm not suggesting you call in the lawyers. But I do think that the more you know about how someone expects to live their life, both spiritually and practically, the more you can decide whether the relationship has a good chance of working for you both.

MOVING IN

Buying a home is a seriously big investment. If you choose to do this, you are going to be making decisions that may involve heavy financial commitment. The fact that two can live more cheaply than one will increase the pressure to join up with someone else and buy or rent. But that's not the only thing to think about. I saw a TV show where the guy moved into his girlfriend's flat. She arrived home to find the place littered with cardboard boxes. He was arranging his stuff in a space that she used for shoe storage. She was horrified. She'd never thought about what she would have to give up to accommodate him and he just assumed he could make space for himself.

The questions below are designed to get you to take some time to think about what you want from your home and be clear about your own needs as well as your partner's. If you are planning on moving in with someone, you would be well advised to get them to think about these things too.

Your Home

- Where do you want to live?
- How do you want that home to be?
- How much space do you need?
- What kind of furniture do you want?
- Make a list of the non-negotiable things you want from your home, the things that you want but are prepared to negotiate over and the things that you consider to be 'icing on the cake'.
- List the benefits and disadvantages of living together.
- If you could afford a place of your own, would you still want to own a joint property or share a full-time home with your partner?

PERSONAL SPACE AND FREEDOM

Some of the biggest complaints couples make is that they don't have 'their space' or that they feel 'tied down'. Often in the first hormone-driven stages of our relationships we are so happy being with the love of our life that our need for personal space seems much less than it really is.

Discussing your needs for personal space could save major hassles later on. Here are some things you might want to think about:

Your Space

Take some time to really think about what's important to you in terms of personal time and space.

- What kind of decisions do you want to make without consulting the other person?
- Do you need your own workroom/study/office?
- How much time alone do you need and when?
- What are your TV watching/radio listening patterns? (My friend Lesley and her husband have agreed no TV in the bedroom, because when he switches on he finds it hard to switch off!)
- Do you want a domain? Some people like to be in charge in the kitchen or the garage.

Some people even feel guilty about wanting time to themselves because they assume that 'people in love want to be together all the time'. This just isn't true in most cases.

Below is a list of some of the things couples do together and on their own. Check off which are ideal for you. And then ask your partner to do the same. Discuss your answers.

During the discussion be prepared to expand on and explain what you specifically mean by your answers.

Activity	Always	Sometimes	Rarely	Never
shopping				
weekends				
meals				
parties				
exercise				
work				
sport				
holidays				
sex				
watching TV				
going out with friends				

HOUSEHOLD CHORES

Personally I think life's too short to vacuum, but I know people who spend hours every day maintaining an immaculate household.

If you are moving in together, working out your expectations about household chores like this can remove the cause of a lot of silly arguments. Sometimes we go into a relationship just expecting men to be good at 'men things' and women to be good at 'women things' and often we're disappointed!

Household Duties

Make a list of common household duties and decide what you would be happy to do and what you don't want to do.

Be specific in your discussions. Deciding who does what won't help unless you are both clear on what you mean by 'clean and tidy' and 'a job well done'. If one of you thinks doing the laundry means shoving it in the washing machine and turning it on and the other thinks it means drying, ironing and folding, you'll be at cross purposes.

When you both do this exploration, you'll also discover whether your expectations are realistic in relation to your partner.

FAMILY, FRIENDS AND HOLIDAYS

Some of the major areas of conflict in relationships are centred around family, friends and holidays! Rather than make the assumption that because you are 'in love' these things will work out, take some time to discuss your attitudes and negotiate how to handle these situations.

It may be that you have always thought that if one of your parents died you'd have the other to live with you. Imagine what would happen if your partner announced that they wanted a parent to move in.

Perhaps you love to take beach holidays while your partner loves to rush around cities.

How are you going to deal with friends now that you are a couple?

Go through the following questions and decide what your thoughts are. Make a list of your answers. Then ask your partner to do the same. Compare notes and discuss areas where you have different ideas.

Family

💜 How often do you expect to visit your family or have them to stay?

💜 Do you expect visiting family to be a joint activity?

Holidays

💜 How do you expect to spend traditional holidays like Christmas, Thanksgiving and Diwali?

💜 What kind of holidays do you like to take?

💜 If your partner wants a different type of holiday, how could you incorporate what you both want and be happy?

💜 Would you be happy to take a separate holiday?

Friends

💜 Do you want to be able to have separate friends?

💜 Do you expect to meet all your partner's friends?

💜 Do you expect your partner to give up certain friends?

💜 How will you handle the dynamics of friendships and a new relationship?

Ex-partners

💜 What kind of relationship do you want to maintain with your exes and how might this affect your partner?

CAREER

Gone are the days when the man worked and the woman stayed at home and the woman followed the man wherever his job took him. Chances are, you've got a career and so has your partner. How will you handle issues that arise from separate careers?

What if your partner were offered a fantastic career opportunity but had to relocate? How would this affect you? What solutions could you come up with? It's far better to think about this now than when you are faced with a decision to make and not much time.

What if one of you loses your job? Would you be prepared/able to support each other and for how long?

People change and it's important to realize that no matter how much you love each other, you won't always necessarily be following the same dreams. Major career changes may involve altered income, working hours and locations. If you have an unfulfilled dream for your life, don't keep it to yourself. Instead discuss your dreams with your partner and consider how this will affect both of you.

MONEY AND ASSETS

I'm not sure that money is the root of all evil, but conflicting attitudes to money can be a major source of problems in a relationship. We get very sensitive when it comes to finance, because we've learned to equate money with power. We may judge people on how much or how little money they spend on various things and on us.

The questions below are designed to make you think about the impact money or lack of it, or mismanagement of it, may have on your relationship.

- ♥ How will you handle money? Are you going to have a joint account, share incomes, keep your finances separate?
- ♥ Who will pay for what?
- ♥ If you live in your partner's house, would you be prepared to pay rent/contribute to upkeep?
- ♥ How will you deal with expenses and bills?
- ♥ If one of you stays at home to look after children, would you treat childcare like a job and expect to be paid for it?
- ♥ What happens if one of you gets into debt? Examine your partner's spending habits and your own and see how they differ.

❤ What happens if one of you dies and you aren't married? Do you think you should include your partner in your will? Should they make provision for you?

When you are clear on all these day-to-day nitty-gritty things, you will feel inclined to spend more time on building and strengthening the emotional side of your relationship.

BUILDING: EVERYDAY RELATIONSHIP MAINTENANCE

Everyone with a smidgen of common sense knows that relationships aren't made in heaven and that a good deal of effort and hard work is required to keep the motor oiled and running smoothly. There are plenty of books that deal with relationship challenges in depth. My intention here is to give you some practical tips for everyday maintenance that are designed to boost the feelgood factor in you and your partner and keep your relationship motor in good working order.

SPREADING YOUR SUNSHINE

'Those that bring sunshine into the lives of others cannot keep it from themselves.'
Sir James M. Barrie

Most of us brighten up when the sun is shining and have to work harder at feeling good when the sky clouds over and darkens. Some people shine so brightly that others love being around them. Others are so miserable and demotivating that everyone avoids them.

Bringing a little sunshine into someone's life is easy and very rewarding, and in a relationship there are a few simple things you can do that will positively bombard your partner with rays of sunshine.

Here are three golden sunshine activities that are guaranteed to boost your relationship.

COMPLIMENTING AND CHEERLEADING

Compliments have so much going for them:

- They don't cost anything.
- They are in unlimited supply.
- They make people feel good.
- They bring a reaction that makes you feel good too.

If you've given out as many as I have, you'll know what it feels like when someone's face transforms into a big smile and you get the buzz back from them as they emit 'feelgood' signals.

Some people don't want to compliment their lovers because they're scared they'll get so big-headed they'll go looking for someone better. But instead of resting on their complimentary laurels, they're more likely to reach for higher standards in the hopes of getting even more compliments!

If you aren't a compulsive complimenter, now's the time to start.

Be Complimentary

- Take a moment or two to look at your lover when they're preoccupied doing something.
- As you gaze, imagine a connection linking your heart to theirs.
- Start making a mental list of all the things you like about them.
- Then tell them.

Compliments are really encouraging and so is cheerleading. Cheerleading is part of American culture, but in many other countries it's not so common. Cheerleading uplifts people to victory. Can you imagine how nice it would be to have someone constantly rooting for you?

Why not start now by doing it for the person you love? It doesn't cost much to say 'Well done' or 'You can do it' or 'I'm so proud of you.'

GET INTO THEIR PASSION

If your lover invites you to share an activity or a passion, or if they want to talk about what they do, be open to it. It's their way of sharing something of themselves with you. There are other benefits too. Through various boyfriends I've learned to shoot a pistol, enjoy football and ride a motorbike. And when you spend time indulging their passion it's more likely to lead to passion in the bedroom later ...

LILY AND OSCAR'S STORIES:
Sharing Passions

Lily loves to be around her man when he watches football. She said, 'He gets so excited, the air is thick with testosterone and he's up for anything afterwards!'

Oscar's girlfriend loves it when he rents a 'chick-flick' and invites her to watch it. He noticed that she gets very cuddly and sexy during these films. By keeping her happy he gets something for himself and the opportunity to make her even happier!

So, instead of criticizing your partner for talking about football or watching weepy movies, make an effort to find out what they like about it and try and see it from their point of view. Your interest is also a sign that you accept them as they are.

'HAVE A GREAT DAY?'

We all have times when we need to air our problems and be listened to. But being in a relationship shouldn't give us a licence to whine and moan as much as we want.

Some of the most sought-after qualities in a partner are confidence, a positive attitude and a happy outlook. Here's a game that will help you develop them.

A Treasure Hunt

Take some time in the evening to look back over the day's events. Imagine you are going on a treasure hunt for all the good things that happened. The train arrived on time, you had a positive conversation with someone at work, you enjoyed your lunch ... Each time something negative comes up, acknowledge it, put it aside and continue your hunt.

Later, take the negative things and find some silver lining in the cloud, for example: 'I got stuck in a traffic jam. The positive side of this is that I was given an involuntary lesson in patience.'

If things have happened that are so bad you want to talk about them to your partner, that's fine. But be sure to talk about it with a purpose to finding a solution rather than just having a moan.

And next time your lover asks, 'How was your day?', tell them about all the good things *first*.

NURTURING YOUR MAN

DON'T MESS WITH A WORK OF ART

We don't buy a precious Old Master to paint over what's already there. But that's just what many women do with their man. When a woman tries to change a man's basic nature, she's telling him he's not OK the way he is.

You can't change someone's basic nature, but you can help them to improve in subtle ways. There's a big difference between cooking healthier food for a man who's overweight and nagging him every time he eats a plate of French fries. When you set a man free to be himself he will flourish in your company and he may absorb a few lessons along the way.

BECOME HIS TREASURED SOURCE OF INTIMACY

Even though guys are programmed to be tough and conceal their emotions, they are still emotional beings and most of them welcome the opportunity to let their hair down and share their challenges and emotions with someone close to them. I'm not saying they want to do this in the way women do, but let them know it's safe to be emotional with you.

Also, show your man that he can remain empowered as he does so. When he begins to talk, pay attention to him as if he is the most fascinating creature in the universe. Be flattered that he is sharing his inner doubts and challenges with you. Remind him of what he's good at and situations he's faced before and resolved. Rather than tea and sympathy and sharing the pain, appeal to the male problem-solving gene and ask him if you can help him find a solution. (And guys, you can take a hint from this. Sometimes a hug or a 'there, there, never mind' is what women are looking for when they're upset, rather than an instant solution!)

ENCOURAGE HIS SEXINESS

Men don't stop fancying other women because they love someone. But being a healthy red-blooded male isn't a crime, so don't treat him like a criminal when you catch him looking – after all, women do it too!

If you see him watching a good-looking woman, let him know that it's OK with a comment like 'I'm not surprised she caught your eye – she's gorgeous.' It will surprise and disarm him.

If he comments on a woman's good looks and you agree, say so. You can't stop what's natural, so you might as well join in.

NURTURING YOUR WOMAN
PROGRAMME HER POSITIVELY

A woman loves to be told that she's beautiful and sexy, but unless you pepper it with other kinds of compliments she's going to worry that your love is only skin deep.

Make sure you comment on her intellectual and emotional qualities too and take the opportunity to programme her to do more of the same by telling her what you love, for example, 'I love the way you take an interest in my work' or 'I love it that I can talk to you about anything.'

If in doubt about what she likes, ask. Rather than attempting, as one of my friends did, to wash your wife's car as a romantic gesture, you'd be better off asking her, 'What's the most romantic thing I can do for you?' Then wait a while and surprise her with it. Don't do it too often, though, as she'll get complacent.

THE REWARDS OF LISTENING

To some men, women sound as if they're babbling in a foreign language when they talk about their emotions. But listening can have major pay-offs. A wise male friend once told me, 'As long as a man thinks he'll get a shag at the end of it, he will listen to a woman for hours.'

Use this method to send her sexy thoughts while she's chattering.

💜 When next she wants to talk, tell her you want to sit opposite her and pay full attention.

💜 Look into her eyes and spend plenty of time maintaining eye contact.

💜 As you listen to her, think about all the great sex you've had. This will send out sexy vibes to her.

💜 As well as feeding back what she's saying to you, you can try this trick. When there's a little gap in her chatter, put your hand on her arm, look her straight in the eyes and swiftly tell her that you love listening to her and how lovely and sexy she is. Make sure you don't distract her, so end your quick interjection by encouraging her to continue. She'll feel great because you're listening and chances are that when she's finished, she'll be open to a bit of what you fancy.

HONOURABLE PERSUASION AND TRAINING

Diplomacy is the art of letting someone else get your own way.

MICHAEL'S STORY:
'A Fairytale Relationship'

Everyone who knows my friend Michael thinks he has a fairytale relationship. But it wasn't always like that.

When Michael and his partner first met they had three basic ingredients: they liked each other, they could talk to each other and they found each other physically attractive.

The rest, he tells me, was all a matter of shaping and 'training'.

I'm not referring to the kind of training that's based on fear, as in 'If I don't get back from the pub the wife'll kill me' or 'I can't wear short skirts because my husband doesn't approve.' That's 'feary scary' stuff. The training I'm talking about involves making an effort to understand and adapt to another person's quirks and habits and using what you know to create win–win situations where you both get something out of it.

We've all heard of the question 'What's in it for me?' Most of us unconsciously ask ourselves that question when asked to do something by someone else. Knowing how to present something in a way that outlines the WIFM for the other person is seriously going to increase your chances of getting them to agree. And if they don't, learn to be OK with 'no'. It's just them making a decision that is right for them at the time.

In an intimate relationship you should know the person well enough to have a handle on their values and priorities. So, if you want someone to help you in some way or join in an activity with you or attend an event, you can organize it so that it appeals to them. Here are some ideas.

USE THEIR STRATEGIES
PETA'S STORY:
'Killing Two Birds with One Stone'

My boyfriend has a thing about 'killing two birds with one stone'. When he plans an outing, he's happiest if he can accomplish as many things as possible in one go. If I want him to come with me somewhere or do something for me, I've found that the best way is to find something that fits in and that's of value to him and sell it to him, for example, 'You could come and stay the night at the hotel with me and then visit your friend nearby while I'm at the seminar.'

If I can't find something of value to use to persuade him, I can just ask and say it's important to me. I can also accept that he might just say no because he has something else to do that's important to him.

Have you ever tried to get your partner to do something but haven't succeeded? Was it because it was really against their values? If not, how did you handle it?

The Art of Persuasion

Reread the section in the last chapter on strategies and what movitates people *(see page 118)*. Try and work out your partner's strategies. For example, if they are motivated to do something by fear of something bad happening – the 'away-from' strategy – use this strategy to persuade them.

- ❤ Think of something you want your partner to do.
- ❤ Think about their particular quirks or strategies.
- ❤ How could you use this to find a different approach?
- ❤ Try it out on something that isn't madly important.
- ❤ If it doesn't work, find another way. Keep noticing what works for them.

MAKE IT JUICY FUN

Everyone has chores they don't really enjoy doing. And sometimes we're faced with what seem like overwhelmingly unpleasant tasks. How can we get through them?

PETA'S STORY:
Tantric Clutter-Clearing

My boyfriend lives in what I shall diplomatically describe as 'a bit of a mess'! He was always complaining about how he wished he could clear it up. This was the inspiration for my 'tantric clutter-clearing programme'.

The idea is to make a chore so much fun that it doesn't seem like a chore at all.

First I got permission. There's nothing more likely to cause discomfort than when someone dives in and starts doing stuff without consulting you first.

Because I know he gets easily distracted, I realized that things could end up even more chaotic as he got drawn into different areas of the clutter. I decided to build in regular distractions in the form of a juicy treat: sex.

I got something out of it because I had built in a treat that I would enjoy too. We spent an hour clearing up and then indulged in some fun and games. And of course one of the key elements of tantric sex is the almost getting there but not quite and building up to the big climax. What was originally planned for one day became so much fun that we spent four days on it.

When you add sex and laughter to a chore, it turns into a game you want to play more of. And when I say now, 'Why don't we arrange another clutter-clearing session?' with that look in my eye, he jumps to it!

LEAD THEM TO WATER

Adults learn best by discovering for themselves. And sometimes we can set things up for our lovers and partners so that they learn in their own way.

If you've read something that you want your partner to read, instead of saying 'You must read this book', you can be much more subtle.

- ♥ Talk about the book and tell them how good it is.
- ♥ Use a highlighter pen to mark the things that are important or meaningful to you.
- ♥ Fold down or bookmark certain pages and leave the book lying somewhere visible and easy for them to pick up. (I left *The Barefoot Doctor's Guide for the Modern Lover* in my boyfriend's bathroom. It led to some interesting experiments in our sex life!)

If they choose to pick it up and read it, fantastic. They'll either be intrigued or not. But at least you're giving them the opportunity.

I'm sure you can see how much more pleasant it is to let someone learn for themselves rather than tell them what you think is true.

What, if anything, do you want to get across to someone? What ways can you come up with of presenting them with this information without telling them? Think creatively.

And remember the old saying 'You can lead a horse to water but you cannot make it drink'. It will always be their choice. Accepting this will make it a lot easier for you!

YOUR PERSONAL WISH FILE

I know that some people have this wonderful knack of being able to buy just the right present for their lover. But others just don't have a clue. Why is it that some men seem to think that your ample hips and bosom are going to fit into a thong designed for an anorexic model? Those that aren't clued in will spend a lot of unwanted time racking their brains to work out what to buy. Men don't ask because they want it to be a surprise and women don't tell them because they expect them to somehow miraculously know. And then the women judge the men for not being in tune with them. Instead of all this game playing we could learn a lot from current wedding-present strategies.

When I'm invited to a wedding or some occasion where gift buying is required, I want to know where the couple are keeping their list. Brides have present lists, so why not keep up the tradition and open your own present list in the form of a file? This file is going to become the repository of all the things you wish for, from presents to anything else you can think of.

Every time you see something you want in a magazine cut it out and put it in the file. Make sure you put it with a note that gives the stockists, phone number, website (if mail order) and price.

Keep a separate piece of paper where you can note down present ideas as they come to you. Write down enough detail so that someone can just go out and buy for you without having to ask any further questions.

Maintain a list of presents that range in price from very inexpensive (could just buy it on a whim) to top budget range (special anniversary presents).

If you buy something for yourself or change your mind about it, remove it from the file.

You can also create separate sections for things like holidays you'd like to go on, or activities or courses you'd like to get into.

If you see an article about erotic massage and it appeals to you, put it in the file with a note saying something like 'This might be fun to try.'

Tell your lover where the file is. And if you don't live together, you can photocopy it and give it to them. You can send it via e-mail. Get creative.

Nowadays we're so busy that we want to spend the little time we have with a lover doing meaningful things. It makes sense to use a file system to make information available so you don't need to tell them about it.

REWARDING WORK
LESLEY'S STORY:
Feeding Him Facts

My friend Lesley is passionate about all aspects of classical music. Her husband Brian likes to listen to it too. Lesley is not just interested in hearing the music, she's fascinated by the history, the details and who plays what. She likes to discuss it with her husband and it's important to her that he knows the title of the music and the composer. So, for example, she will say, 'Let's go and see Isserlis play Elgar's cello concerto next week.'

Brian's happy to find out more, but he responds much more readily if it's laid out on a plate for him. Lesley knows this strategy and uses it by finding a situation where she can feed him facts and reward him if he gets them right.

When they're on their way home, listening to music in the car, she feeds him all the facts. He then has to prove he's learned them by repeating them. And if he gets it right he gets a blow job as soon as they get home! Everyone's happy, Lesley can talk to her husband about the music they both love, they listen to music and their sex life gets spiced up into the bargain. Nice deal!

What do you want your partner to learn about? Are they willing to learn? If they can't be bothered to learn, how can you teach them in a way that's rewarding to both of you? What games can you devise and what rewards can you offer?

Remember, sex isn't a dog biscuit. If you offer it as a reward for certain types of behaviour, make sure it's offered in addition to what you normally do and that it's not withheld when the person doesn't learn. 'Punishment' doesn't exist in my book.

THE GENTLE ART OF REFRAMING
SEEING IT ANOTHER WAY

I don't think there are bad situations or good situations. I think there are just situations. How we react is what makes a situation good or bad. Most of us are trained to seek out the bad and react to that. How about seeing things another way?

When you find other ways of looking at events, it can completely change your thoughts and reactions. It can make the difference between feeling awful and feeling very good.

'If you see someone's clothes lying on the floor don't think, "Mess," think, "Someone's naked in here," and get excited!'
Richard Bandler

I agree. How about you? Is there anything you need to 'reframe'?

Think of something that you consider to be a fault in your partner.

For example: *He's too critical.*

And think of ways in which being critical can be useful.

He picks out the mistakes and then I can correct them.

He's a good driver because he notices everything that goes on around him.

She's too untidy

At least if I have something out of place when she visits, she's not going to think badly of me.

Maybe I could help her to tidy up in a fun way and she could do something for me in return.

Her mind is too occupied with wonderful dreams to be tidy and I'd rather she dreamed and was happy than was tidy and miserable.

Do this with as many faults as you can think of.

LAUGH AND THE WORLD LAUGHS WITH YOU

'Anyone without a sense of humour is at the mercy of everyone else.'

William Rotsler

A secure person knows their strengths – and their limitations. Their confidence allows them to laugh at the things they aren't quite so good at, reframing them into a positive situation – or one they can make fun of, at least.

Being able to laugh at yourself also gives other people permission to join in.

The Comedy Star

Think of something 'klutzy' you did in the past where you didn't react with a laugh.

Imagine you're watching yourself in a movie and you're the star comedian. You win an Oscar for your role.

You are at the awards ceremony and they are playing a scene from your movie. It's where you are doing the silliest, most embarrassing thing you can imagine. See yourself acting out this role and making other people laugh. And see yourself being handed the Oscar and everyone cheering you.

And then step into the movie and really enjoy the sensation of being in front of that crowd.

Your award is for the King or Queen of Comedy.

'Why look back and laugh about it when you can laugh about it now?'
Richard Bandler

Of course there is loving fun-poking and resentful fun-poking. If you are laughing at someone else, there are times when some sensitivity is called for. Only laugh at someone in loving fun.

REVIEWING

What comes to mind when you hear those words 'We have to talk'? Sometimes they are said in that tone and with that look that means that things have gone too far.

Sometimes the 'We have to talk' phase comes way after the time when you should have been talking. I know, I've been there myself. And all that time all the things that have been left unsaid have been bubbling up inside and then they explode in an unpleasant and messy way.

So instead of waiting until the explosion, or, as many people do, having to sort out your relationship with the help of a counsellor, how about reviewing it on a regular basis? If you have a regular health check up, it's easy for the doctors to catch something before it gets too big to handle. Frequent relationship reviews can be very useful in the same way.

If you think about it, we're always reviewing our relationships. But sometimes we review them from the wrong side. We look at what's wrong first instead of looking at what's right. After all, if you make yourself aware of what's good, it's much easier to look more calmly on what isn't working right now.

Before you begin to review a relationship, it might be useful to review yourself. You can do this on a daily, weekly or any regular basis that works for you. It might help to keep a diary. Again, your choice.

Reviewing Yourself and your Partner

Ask these review questions of yourself for the period since your last review and then review your partner in the same way. Mark yourself on a scale of 1–10, with 1 being 'not nearly good enough' and 10 being 'excellent, do more of this'.

- How affectionate have I been?
- How complimentary have I been?
- How grateful have I been?
- How well have I controlled emotions like anger, jealousy, resentment?
- What special things have I done for the other person?
- What efforts have I made to spice up our sex life?
- How good a listener have I been?
- What could I improve on in the next period?

You can also ask:

- What have I left unsaid that needs to be addressed?
- What would I like to discuss with my partner at our review meeting?

INCOMPLETIONS

Sometimes we go through life promising we'll do more of this or less of that and then carry on just as we were. And sometimes we want to say something and we don't. How many of these have you wanted to do but not done yet – apologies, explanations, encouragement, praise, listening, asking for something, surprising, sharing bad news, resolving arguments, finishing discussions ...? What else can you think of?

When we want to do something and don't take care of it, it is like having a drawer full of overdue bills. I call these 'incompletions'.

Completing Incompletions

♥   What incompletions would you like to complete today/this week/this month? Set yourself a target to do them before your next review.

♥   What roles have you been playing that made you feel off centre or not yourself? List the positive purpose of this role-playing and also list the negative side-effects.

♥   What niggles do you have about your partner that have gone unsaid? Are you expecting them to be something you never agreed on in the first place?

♥   What would you like to discuss with them?

♥   When would be a good time to do this?

By completing as many of your incompletions as possible, you'll find out how cleansing and refreshing it can be.

EIGHT KEYS TO REVIEWING

1. Do it before the problems start and do it regularly.
2. Pick a time and location that suits you both and set a time limit.
3. Prepare your 'agenda'. Have a list of items you want to discuss and prioritize them. Know what you want and what's in it for your partner, and be flexible.
4. Agree that each of you will have a turn to talk while the other listens. Questions can be asked at the end.
5. Start out with loving feelings. Remind them of something nice that you've shared or something positive they've done in the past.
6. Own your statements. You might say, for example: 'When you do …, I feel …'
7. Create joint responsibility and encourage a joint solution: 'What can we do about that?'
8. Agree on who will do what and set a time for another review.

REVIEW GAMES

Likes, Niggles and More Likes

Sometimes it's good to remind each other about what you like about them. I like this game because it's easily done in a few minutes and as a bonus, it allows you to sandwich things that niggle you in between things that you really like and the person will get the message without getting upset! It's like taking nasty medicine with a sugar coating.

- Sit opposite your lover so that you can make eye contact.
- Decide who's going to be 'the speaker' first and who 'the asker'.
- Make eye contact.
- The asker then asks the speaker the following questions:

  'What do you like most about me?'

  'What, if anything, do I do that niggles you?'

  'What's the thing you like most of all about this relationship?'
- As the speaker replies, the asker just listens. No comments, no questions. (It's much more powerful if the speaker looks the asker in the eye.)
- When the speaker finishes, the asker thanks them.
- Then you change over and repeat the process.
- You should both feel very warm towards each other when you've finished.
- Afterwards thank each other and have a hug or share a drink or whatever takes your fancy ...

Five-Minute Homework

My friend Ralphie and his girlfriend are both busy professionals with punishing schedules. They play this game on a daily basis as a way of making sure they communicate regularly.

- You get five (vary it to suit you) minutes each to speak about anything you want to.
- While one person is speaking, the other person cannot comment or ask questions, they just listen.
- When both have had a turn, if you still feel you need more time or want to discuss something further, you agree to continue or set a time to do so.

Ralphie told me that this game really opened out their communication and taught them the art of just being there for each other, if only for five minutes.

STEPPING INTO THEIR SHOES

'Never judge a man till you've walked a mile in his moccasins.'

Lao Tse

Sometimes we get upset because our lover can't see our point of view and doesn't appear to understand what we're feeling. If this resonates with you, the chances are that your partner may feel the same.

When you metaphorically step into someone's shoes it helps you to experience their view of the world and get more understanding of their motives. It also enables you to see yourself through their eyes, hear what you say through their ears and get a sense of what they are feeling.

Stepping into their Shoes ...

This exploration is designed to get you to physically shift into someone else's experience.

- Mark out three positions on the floor. You can use paper if you want to or just imagine three circles. The positions are 'Me', 'Them' and 'Observer'.
- Recall a conflict you had with your partner.
- Start in the 'Me' position and play it through as if you are reliving it from your own point of view. What were the main issues for you?
- Remind yourself why you still love this person.
- Now step into the 'Them' position. Imagine you are your lover looking at you in the 'Me' position. Stand the way they stand and imagine stepping into their energy.
- Then ask what might be going on for them.
- Come up with one or more good reasons why having things go their way would have made them feel better.
- What do you think they wanted from you?
- What might they be thinking about you and the things you said?
- Now think of your last meal (just to change your state).
- And step into the 'Observer' position.

- ♥ Look at yourself and the other person. What do you think a neutral observer might see going on between the two of you?
- ♥ What gestures were you making towards each other? What were you saying to each other? What, as an observer, does your intuition tell you about these two people?

I know it sounds a little crazy, but it's surprising how just shifting into another mode and using your imagination can allow you to see, feel and hear things differently and sometimes much more clearly.

Whenever there is something that you and your partner disagree about or need to resolve, take the time to do this exercise. It may give you some new ideas. It will certainly increase your empathy for your partner.

You can apply this to any area of your life where you need to step back and see things from someone else's position.

LAURA'S STORY:
Stepping into the Good Times

Laura was having problems in her relationship. She and her boyfriend had been together for two years and now they were arguing more and not having as much fun. When she talked to me about it, I asked her if she was still the person he fell in love with.

I got her to spend some time thinking about those early days while concentrating on the feelings, sounds and looks that went on between them then. I asked her to imagine stepping from herself now into herself then and to experience it through her own eyes, not as an observer. I advised her to do this on a regular basis for a week and notice the difference.

She wrote to me to tell me how it worked out for her.

'When I stepped back into the "old me" I remembered the feelings I had whenever I saw him, when I anticipated seeing him, when I listened to him, when we went out, when we touched. I remembered how I must have looked to him – with bright eyes, a happy walk, smiling, spontaneous movements – and what noises I made – laughing, agreeable, interested and sexy noises – and I thought, "*That's* the person he fell in love with!"

She didn't tell him what she'd been doing, but was delighted when a week later, he said, "You've been different this week, more like how you were when we first met." '

The beauty of this system is that it puts control in *your* hands rather than you just hoping that the other person will change or do something to perk up the relationship.

A WORD ABOUT SEX

SEXY FLIRTING

People flirt for all kinds of reasons and some people don't flirt at all. Give yourself a pat on the back if you can say with a smile: 'I *love* flirting and I do it often.'

I'm always surprised by the number of people who tell me that they don't flirt any more because they're in a relationship. Flirting isn't just for singles seeking a mate, it's a wonderful way of deepening and maintaining contact with someone you really care for.

Flirting can be done at any time with anyone. And it can be as low-key nice or as juicily sexy as you want it to be. And talking of juicy sexy flirting, the most wonderful time to flirt with full abandon and as wildly or as coyly as you want is when you flirt with someone you are already intimate with.

If you are in a relationship and you don't flirt with your partner, now is a good time to start.

Most people love to be flirted with when it's done well and with honest meaning behind it, whether it's 'I want to shag you' or 'I like your caring attitude.' If you don't flirt with your partner, they might be drawn to someone who does flirt with them and that could be dangerous.

You know a lot of intimate stuff about your partner, which means that you can use some of it to start some really sexy flirting. Here are my four sexy flirting tips:

1. **Remind them of the good stuff.**
    When you part, for the day or for a week or longer, remember a particularly juicy scene from your sex life and pick out the bit they moaned and groaned at the

most. Get really close to them and whisper into their ear, 'Mmm, I'm just thinking about how ...' Finish it with an 'Mmmmmmm' in a very sexy voice. Next time you see them you might only have to whisper the 'Mmmmmm' to send them right back into the experience. Now how useful is that?

2. **Remind them of what's to come.**

Here's a great one if you are going out for an evening where you'll be socializing separately. It reminds me of the words of that song about being able to dance any dance but remembering later who's taking you home and in whose arms you're going to be. This works on the same premise. You accept that both you and your partner can flirt with anyone and flirt wantonly, as long as you remember the juicy treat that is to come: flirting (and more) with each other.

Before you go out, tell your partner about what you want to do to them that evening or the next morning (and make sure you can do it, i.e. you won't be too drunk, tired, etc). Build up the picture till they're very excited. And then snog them with as much passion as you're feeling. And as you finish, say the word 'Later ...'

Throughout the evening you will encounter them as you flit around the room. If necessary, put a hand on their shoulder or bum or wherever to get their attention. Whisper, 'Later ...' as you look them deep in the eyes, and move on. It's sooooo tantalizing and it'll keep you in their mind no matter whom they flirt with or who flirts with them.

3. **Use your body.**

This is a simple one. They've got a favourite body part of yours, haven't they? When you are at home or together for any period of time and you feel yourselves sinking into domestic boredom, expose that body part to them in a very sexy way, whisper what you'd like them to do to you there, or, if they're really touchy feely, take their hand and subtly place it there.

You can also share a sexy fantasy with them in the commercial break while you are watching TV. Keep injecting sex into general everyday life and you'll keep their flames burning for you.

4. **Use technology.**

When you are apart, if it is appropriate, ring, e-mail or text occasionally. When they go away, put a sexy picture of yourself or some reminder of the good times into their case. Slip a postcard into a jacket pocket or a handbag. I found a great postcard that said: 'I feel sexy.' I turned up at my boyfriend's place and waved the card in front of him. He got the message!

Keep your communication sexy and short! Don't use a regular pattern like always ringing at 4.30 p.m. – the surprise goes and it just becomes an everyday occurrence.

SEEING, HEARING AND FEELING IT
DEENA'S STORY:
All Sorts of Great Times

Deena is a very touchy feely woman. Her former lover used to like looking at her when they made love. She was always a little conscious of her wobbly bits, even though he didn't seem to notice. He used to *take pictures* of her and commented how much he liked the *brown colour* of her nipples as opposed to rosy pink ones. He liked her to wear sexy *lacy underwear.*

Her next lover was very different. One of the first things he said to her when she squealed as he brushed her nipples was: 'I love the way *you respond to my touch*ing your nipples.' When Deena wore her lacy underwear with him, he wasn't particularly impressed. One day she put on a silky top and pants. He remarked on *how soft her body felt* through the material. When they discussed it they realized that although he liked the look of the lacy underwear, *he didn't like the harsh feel* of it.

Deena had also had a relationship with a musician. He loved to be slapped with a ruler when he was coming. Deena thought he liked the burning sensation of the slap until he explained it wasn't the feel, but the *sound* of the ruler hitting his skin that turned him on. She also realized that when he wanted her to talk dirty to him, he always insisted on her doing it in a particular voice. He knew just which *tone turned him on.*

Although Deena was more naturally in synch with her touchy-feely lover, her flexibility helped her to enjoy a good sex life with men whose sense-ual preferences were different from hers.

We all sense the world in different ways. Some of us will be more visual, like Deena's first lover, others more touchy feely and others more auditory. We have already seen how this is reflected in our speech.

When you know what is your lover's preferred sense it serves three purposes:

1. It might explain why they are the way they are.
2. It might help you to be aware of areas where you may clash.
3. It might make you aware of which sense you need to develop to be more in harmony/blend more easily with/get more in touch with your partner.

DEREK AND NATHALIE'S STORY:
'I Need You to ...'

When Derek and Nathalie realized that they were going to take their relationship to another stage and that in some way they were committed to each other, they wanted to make sure that they understood each other's needs and wants. As part of their discussions, they asked each other the question: *'What do you need me to do to show my love?'*

Derek told Nathalie that he wanted her to touch him. He suggested that a hand on the shoulder or a rub on the back on a regular basis would be all that he needed to reassure him of her love.

Nathalie, on the other hand, wanted to hear things from Derek. She said, 'I just want you to tell me nice things from time to time.' Derek wasn't sure what she meant. Nathalie suggested he tell her that she looked good or that she smelt nice.

From one simple question, both of them learned something that was core to the other's feeling loved.

This isn't being needy, it's a naturally nice thing to want and to give to someone. The key is to discover in what format they want these gestures.

Nathalie told me later that the first time Derek tried this out he got into bed and said, 'You know, Nathalie, you don't smell.' She couldn't stop laughing. Derek, poor thing, thought that by telling her she didn't smell *bad*, she would feel good. She put him right and now he's quick to whisper from time to time, 'You smell *lovely*, Nathalie.'

HOW TO BE THE BEST LOVER IN THE WORLD!

❤ Find out what your partner's preferred sense is and try to experience the world from that sense.

♥ Be sure to ask that crucial question: *'What do you need me to do to show my love?'*

♥ And be sure to tell them what *you* need from *them*.

It's also good to be a friend to your lover. John Gottman, a psychologist at the University of Washington-Seattle, reckons that friendship in a relationship leads to better sex. Although some people report having great sex after an almighty row, this is dangerous because it builds a link between rowing and sex. What is likely to happen is that you will unconsciously generate a row in order to have great sex. It's better to be friends!

Gottman suggests that the way for a man to connect really well with a woman is to:

'Make efforts to understand how she thinks and what motivates her. Be affectionate; tell her what you like about her; show her respect. Open out emotionally.'

IF YOU WANT SOMETHING, GIVE IT AWAY OR ASK FOR IT!

Women often complain that men don't spend enough time on foreplay. One way to encourage him is to do it for him first! When he realizes how much pleasure he gets from your languid and drawn out attentiveness, he will be more encouraged to do the same for you. And you'll probably get off on giving him pleasure as much as he enjoys receiving it!

If your partner wants to indulge in a sexual fantasy, be open. Think of it as a game and have fun acting it out. By indulging their fantasies, there's much more chance they'll want to act out yours. In fact, they're probably desperate to find out what you want so that they can satisfy you.

One of the things that turns most people on sexually is when they are helping someone else to have immense pleasure. We all love to hear, see, feel our partner have a rip-roaring time. And sometimes it's easy to spend so much time on someone else that you don't allow yourself all that you want. Are you always giving the gifts or do you get them too? Surrender to your own desires, be open to theirs, be clear about what you really want and let them have the pleasure of giving you pleasure.

If you want sex, don't always wait for the other person to initiate it, let them know you want them in no uncertain terms. Naturally, you should be mindful of their moods, as they should be of yours. And you've probably heard this before, but I'm going to remind you: the fact is that most healthy balanced men feel flattered when a woman initiates sex. Imagine what it is like having to to do all of the asking. After a while you might begin to wonder if the other person is interested at all.

When you truly enjoy your lover, you will see sexuality not as submission but as a surrender to your highest desires and a wonderful way of spending time. As a result your partner's desire will increase and magic will happen.

HOW TO GIVE THE BEST ORAL SEX IN THE WORLD

Sorry, this isn't a magic technique. There are a load of books out there with reams of information on how to give great oral sex. And several of them have some very useful basic advice. But when it comes down to the nitty gritty, what's right for one person isn't always right for another. And everyone knows what they really like.

So, if you want to give great oral sex, follow this advice:

- First tell them that you want to do it right for them and get them to co-operate by giving you clear feedback.
- Then ask, ask, ask, ask, ask, try, try, try, try ...
- And keep doing it until they give you a sign that you're getting it right ...

BE OPEN TO NEW IDEAS

If your partner tries to introduce you to things you've not yet tried, before you refuse, ask yourself: 'What can I learn from being open, be curious and adventurous?'

Make it clear what you do and don't like – but not before you try things out or consider how they could be adapted so that you both enjoy it.

ENDINGS AND BEGINNINGS

GETTING OVER IT

Twenty years ago my partner died in a car crash. From the moment of being told about the accident to the funeral and way beyond I was carried along on a wave of kindness and sympathy.

If that same partner had left me for another woman, do you think for a moment that I'd have received the outpouring of sympathy and concern from all those people for such a long time? I think not. Sure, my close girlfriends would have listened and sympathized, but somehow there is a stigma still attached to a partner leaving that generates different attitudes.

Eighteen years later I mentioned the death of my partner to someone and they were profuse in their sympathy. I have long since healed, but it made me think. I wonder if that person would have even dreamt of expressing her sorrow had I told her that my partner left me 20 years ago. I suspect she'd think I should have got over it by now! Strange how we work, isn't it?

When a loved one dies, there is a finality. We know that they didn't leave us for someone else, so it seems easier to feel honoured and loved. When a loved one leaves, especially when they leave for or quickly find someone else and we have not, the loss is even more tearing because we know they are out there. There is no finality. There is always the possibility that somehow we can put together the pieces.

Both types of loss share common factors. The person you loved is no longer in your life. Your grief can be as deep when someone leaves you as when they die.

It seems to me that we don't give the same degree of concern and care to those whose lover has left them as we do to those whose lover has died. When someone leaves, we need to go through the same process of grieving, acceptance and moving on as we would if that person had died. We need to create our own sense of finality so that we can move on, and we need the sympathy and tender support of our friends.

So, how do you get over it? What do you need to do in order to heal quickly and move on with a smile on your face and hope for the future?

Accept your sadness and be very, very kind to yourself.

Do not put undue pressure on yourself. Take time off from work if necessary. During this mourning period, learn to accept that this person was put in your path for you both to learn and grow and remember the good things and value them. Buy books or attend workshops that support the idea of letting go and feeling good about yourself. Ask your doctor to recommend a grief counsellor if that feels right. You are just as entitled to one as someone who has lost a loved one to death.

CREATE A FAREWELL RITUAL

When someone dies we have formal funerals, but when a loved one leaves we have no such comforting ritual. That's why it might help to create your own.

A ritual can be anything that marks out a stage in life. A ritual to mark the end of a relationship might be lighting a candle and saying, 'I let you go and wish you well and I welcome love into my life.' It might be going out into the countryside and letting out an almighty scream … or burying love letters and saying a few words of farewell.

If you can, burn love letters and things that remind you of what is no more. Letting go of the material goods helps to let go of the memory. Don't be tempted to keep souvenirs and pore over them – it will only make the memory linger on.

Maybe it's time to have a funeral and get your own closure. I don't mean to be morbid about this. But sometimes burying stuff and saying a goodbye prayer or some uplifting words can work wonders.

TOM'S STORY:
Burying the Memory

When Tom's wife left him for her lover, he was devastated. They had no children and no reason to contact each other, but he couldn't let go of her. I advised him to bury the memory, literally.

He bought a small box from a gift shop and in it he put a picture of himself and his wife, his wedding ring and some other mementoes he'd been holding on to. We took the box to a place where they'd had lots of fun together, which happened to be the pier at Brighton. We decided on a burial at sea. Tom weighted the box down with a heavy stone from the beach. We stood at the end of the pier and he said a few words of farewell. He thanked his wife for the time they'd had together and wished her well. Then he threw the box into the sea. And then we went to the pub and got drunk!

Tom tells me that it was much easier after that to put aside painful thoughts of his wife and think about what was possible for him now and in the future.

Do whatever feels right for you. (For more on this, see Resources.)

TREAT YOURSELF

All the books and experts tell you this, because it's good for you.

Food might be the first treat that comes to mind, but be moderate. Stop counting calories and allow your body to tell you what to eat.

Think of the type of exercise you would most love to do and start doing it.

Another old standby is your bath. Buy some aromatic bath oil, light loads of candles and soak for as long as you need.

Read a book like *A Woman's Worth* by Marianne Williamson or hunt the bookshops for a book on getting over it. There are plenty around.

If the fancy takes you, spend time making love to yourself and really enjoying it. Buy a sex toy, look at things that turn you on. Even though you have lost a lover, there is no need to stop loving yourself. Keeping your sexual fires stoked produces feelgood chemicals in your body and is very healing.

Here are a few more ideas.

Count your Blessings

Ask yourself each day what you have to be grateful for. Thinking that you have a roof over your head or a job or that you have friends or family who love you is sometimes very healing. Be grateful that you have enough to eat. Be grateful for sunshine.

Remember You're Great!

Make a list of all the things that are great about you. Say out loud: 'What I like about myself is ...'

You're such a good deal! Make a list of all the good qualities a lover will get when they get you. Read it often. Add to it whenever you think of something else.

Go on a Personal Development Workshop

This will boost your positive self-image. You'll also meet new people who are also trying to improve their lives and they are likely to have positive attitudes that will uplift and inspire you.

Surround Yourself with People Who Give You Hope

Avoid people who pat you on the back and say stuff like 'Oh how awful' and seek out people who say things like 'So what's next? What wonderful new people are out there who are going to be just right for you?'

And when you are looking back at yourself from the future, having got over it, what would you tell yourself that you have learned? Make it something worthwhile.

'LET'S BE FRIENDS'

Most of us have either said those words or had them said to us. They might mean 'I don't want to be your lover, I just like you as a friend.' They usually mean 'Let's stop being lovers and just be friends.' Making this transition is usually easier when both people are happy to let go and move on. But not all relationships end this way.

When a relationship breaks up usually one person wants it to happen and one doesn't. This means painful emotions are going to surface – sadness, hurt, resentment, bitterness... Need I go on? Until these emotions have been worked through, it will be difficult to form a truly open and honest relationship. And it may take time.

Once you have both been able to forgive, learn the lesson, let go and move on, however, the relationship can move to wonderful levels. Sometimes people become good friends with their ex's new lovers. All kinds of friendships can develop, but they are dependent on the maturity, self-worth and attitude of everyone concerned.

LIAM AND ARLENE'S STORY:

Being Friends

Liam made the choice to leave Arlene and she was very hurt. When he left she said, 'I hope we can still be friends.'

Liam wanted a friendship too, but because he wasn't hurting as much as Arlene, he knew it wouldn't work. He deliberately avoided making contact because he suspected Arlene would take this as renewed interest. Arlene wasn't happy with this and accused him of not wanting to be friends at all. But he somehow knew she needed more time to heal and wasn't ready for friendship.

A year later Liam met Arlene at a party. She was with a new man and appeared very happy. They agreed to have lunch and thus began a friendship that has been going strong now for 10 years.

Sometimes people need time to heal before a real friendship can develop.

Sometimes they aren't ready to be friends until they've found someone new.

Sometimes they pretend to be friends but make it clear they don't want to know about any new lovers. If this is the case, they're probably not over the relationship yet.

I believe:

Good friends shouldn't feel obliged to share everything, but they shouldn't deliberately hide things either.

Good friends care about each other and want the best for them, even if it does mean developing an intimate relationship with someone else.

If you want to be true friends with an ex-lover, doing the following exploration will tell you whether you are ready or not.

How Honest is your Friendship?

If you have a lover who wants to be friends but you are a little cautious, asking these questions and imagining how they really feel might clarify things for you.

If they are leaving or have left you:

- Are you seeking friendship for the children's sake?
- Can you accept why they must leave and let them go?
- Does that person give you something you can't get elsewhere?
- Are you able to say truthfully that if they find someone else you'll be happy for them?
- How do you want the friendship to operate? How often do you want to see them? Do you only want to see them on their own? What else?

If you are leaving them:

- Do you feel they still need you emotionally?
- Do you feel guilty about leaving?
- Do you think that if you give them some time they'll get over it more quickly?
- Do you think that if you see them they'll have more hope?
- How do you think they will handle your being with someone else?
- Would you like to be friends with them?

Now, given what you know about the situation, what's the best course of action?

NEW BEGINNINGS

You may be embarking on a new relationship or you may have just left or been left by someone you loved and learned from. You may have reached another level with someone you already like and love. Whatever is true for you, remember that you are just passing through a stage on the adventure of your life. What's next?

Perhaps you want to spend some time re-affirming your own natural self and adding in the lessons you've learned … and looking forward to the next stage and opening out to new relationships and ways of loving.

A FINAL WORD

I truly believe that all of us are on this Earth to uncover who we really are and to learn the lessons that help us grow. My aim with this book was to help you understand yourself and overcome some of the programming that we have all been subjected to and to develop a more natural and fun way of relating to other people.

The first part of the process is to become aware that there is more to life than the way it is right now, and this applies whether you are blissfully happy or sadly despondent. The next stage is to recognize what is stopping us. When we know that, we are able to do the work that will open us out to all the possibilities in store for us … including meaningful and positive relationships. And then we can use all our skills of flirtatious and loving communication to make it a relationship that's fun and rewarding to be in.

None of this will happen if you are not prepared to put in the effort to make the changes. So I shall leave you with the thought that you alone can do that and it's your choice whether you want to stay as you are or move on to the next stage of your adventure.

Enjoy the rest of your life.

Spread the word: If you purchased this book on Amazon or one of the internet book sites and you enjoyed it, please take the time to review it. Thanks and big smiles from Peta.

RELATIONSHIP QUESTIONNAIRE

These explorations are designed to make you think about what you believe currently about various aspects of relationships. You can also work through them with your partner to find out more about what they think.

Your Beliefs about Marriage

- Write a paragraph stating 'I want to get married/I got married because ...' or 'I don't want to get married because ...'
- What does marriage mean to you? Think of the first 10 words that come up and write them down. Read each word separately and as you do, check your feelings.
- What fantasies, hopes and meaning do you attach to marriage?
- What beliefs do you have about marriage?
  Which of these are of your own making? Which are from your parents, your religion or the media?
- If you want/had a religious wedding, is this because you are religious or is it just part of the dream package along with the white dress?

- Do you feel marriage gives you something you don't have in your life?
  Security? You've nabbed someone or you've found someone to look after you?
  Status? 'I'm married … that means I'm something special'?
  Stability? Marriage makes you more responsible …?
  What else?
  How will you get those things if your spouse leaves you? Do you have any contingency plans?
- What comes to mind when you think about pre-nuptial agreements and relationship contracts?
- If you want to or did marry for love, what will/did marriage do for you?
- Do you see the wedding day as the happiest day of your life?
  If so, does that mean nothing as wonderful can ever happen again?
  How does that limit you?
- If you are married, what's the reality now compared to what you expected when you got wed?

Your Beliefs about Children

Examine carefully your thoughts and remember that as you grow and change your beliefs and needs may change too.

- Do you truly want children?
- What will having children give you?
- What will not having them give you?
- What have you got to offer them?
- Do you have fixed ideas about what gender and how many? How might this affect you if it doesn't work out like that?
- With whom do you want them? A friend, a partner?
- Is there something you have to be doing before you have children?
- How much compromise are you prepared to make in your own life to have children?
- If you want children and then discover you can't have them,
  How would this affect you?
  How else could you be fulfilled?

❤ Make a list with two columns. On one side put all the benefits of having children and on the other side put all the benefits of not having children.

And if you are already thinking of having children with someone, please do yourself a favour and find out what they think. It will help you both clarify what you want.

Your Beliefs about Monogamy

❤ What constitutes being 'unfaithful' in your book?
   Is it kissing someone else or is it a full-blown long-term affair or something in between?
   How important is it to you that someone is sexually faithful?
❤ Have you made a pact with your partner about monogamy?
❤ Have you ever expected them to be unfaithful but not discussed it?
   What stopped you discussing it?
❤ How did this affect your relationship?
❤ What are you prepared to accept and what can't you accept? Get clear on what you want and convey it.
❤ Are you able to abide by the terms you lay down for someone else?
   Know what you want and go for it and be honest about it.

Your Beliefs about Commitment

❤ Write down 10 words that come to mind when you think of commitment. Don't censor them.
   Look at each word and check your feelings.
   Are they positive or are they a bit uncomfortable? You'll know which ones you have to get clear on.
❤ If you ask someone to commit to you, what are you asking them to do? Be as detailed as you want.
❤ If you are prepared to commit to someone, what are you willing to do?
❤ What's the biggest commitment you can make to someone? Is it marriage, living together, buying a house, being monogamous, promising to take on their children, being prepared to look after them if they are sick?

- If you are in a committed relationship, what restrictions are there on your activities? What restrictions do you place on your partner's activities? Are you both truly happy with this?
- If you are in a relationship, what freedoms do you want and what freedoms are you happy for the other person to have?
- What would it be like to be free and to be committed to someone at the same time?
- Is there someone in your life that you're chaining down?
- Is someone trying to hold you back?

  If so, are you prepared to stick with it for now or would it be better to end the relationship?

Your Values

You can do the following exploration on the values that you came up with earlier (*see page 105*). It will help you get clear on what you mean by them. And it'll be mighty useful when you come to discuss them with someone close to you.

I'm going to use 'integrity' as an example.

- What does integrity mean to you? Does a person have to be true to themselves or do they have to mean what they say or what?
- What evidence will prove to you that someone has 'integrity'?
- How do you demonstrate integrity?
- What does someone have to do for you to consider them lacking in integrity?

  You might like to ask the same questions about:

  commitment

  respect

  honesty

  trust

  love

  fidelity

  romance

What's Most Important?

It's often useful to know what's most important to you. There are some things you absolutely must have, others you want but don't need, and yet others that would be nice but aren't necessary.

💜 Get back in touch with your 'yes/no' signals (*see pages 20–22*).

💜 Now look at each item on your values list separately.

💜 When you get the 'yes' signal, put a circle round the item.

💜 Whittle the list down to 10 by comparing each one in turn.

💜 Mark each of the 10 on a scale of 1 to 5, where 5 means 'absolutely must have', somewhere in the middle means 'would like quite a lot', and 1 means 'nice but not necessary at all'.

💜 Look at the three highest-scoring items

Which is top of the list?

How about starting there and working down?

This will help you to clarify what are your most important values.

💜 What qualities do you want from a partner in a relationship?

💜 Make a list randomly without thinking about them.

💜 Check whether any seem to be heading-type categories and which may be details about that particular heading, i.e. 'I want great sex' in contrast to 'I want someone who is good at oral sex.' Great sex means many things to many people, whereas good at oral sex is a lot more specific. You can get even more specific than that. And the more you specify details, the harder it is going to be to find someone to match your requirements.

RESOURCES

Learning a skill is like opening a doorway. Though the door can be opened by another, each person must continue the journey for themselves if they are to attain mastery of that skill.

Now that the internet has opened so many doors, it's easy to find almost any book you want. Nearly all of the books mentioned can be ordered through amazon.co.uk or amazon.com without knowing the ISBN number or the publisher.

HIGHLY RECOMMENDED

The books, tapes and courses listed below have been major turning-points in my development and my way of thinking. They have profoundly affected my life. I heartily recommend them.

Carol Adrienne, *The Purpose of your Life*
If you in any way feel that you have a purpose in life that you have not yet discovered, or if indeed you do have a purpose and want to be sure about it, this book will guide you through a process of self-discovery that is truly empowering.

Richard Brodie, *Virus of the Mind*
If you want to know more about how people are mentally programmed by ideas and how to programme yourself for more useful beliefs, read this book!

Dr Larry Dossey, *Be Careful What You Pray For – You Might Get It*
Larry Dossey, an American medical doctor, examines the hefty evidence in favour of the power of thought to hex and also to cure. If you are in any way interested in how belief systems are formed and how powerful your words can be, read this book. It may save your life, or someone else's.

George Leonard and Michael Murphy, *The Life We Are Given*
A truly comprehensive personal development programme for those who are in it for the long term, this has produced some amazing changes in people over a year-long period.

Diane K. Osborn (ed.), *Reflections on the Art of Living: A Joseph Campbell Companion*
This book presents the basic philosophy that has influenced my work. A treasure trove of ways of living that allow you to flourish as *you*. A wonderful book.

Candace Pert, *Molecules of Emotion*
Candace Pert proved scientifically that emotion can be formed in cell structures – that we do indeed form 'molecules of emotion'. A useful reference for the scientifically minded and an interesting story of a woman's struggle in the male-dominated world of science.

James Redfield, *The Tenth Insight: An Experiential Guide*
You don't have to have read *The Celestine Prophecy* to learn from this book. It is a fully-rounded self-help book that helped me through some challenging times.

Barbara Sher, *Wishcraft*
This was the first book that really opened me out to the possibilities that I can live the life I love and love the life I live. I recommend all her other books too.

Neale Donald Walsch, *Conversations with God*
In this worldwide bestseller, Walsch has opened to the world at large the thoughts that many of us have had for years. There is more out there, and there are better ways of living. I recommend the whole *Conversations with God* series.

Marianne Williamson, *A Return to Love*
Read this book and learn how to be more loving of yourself and others. A true gem.

Marianne Williamson, *A Woman's Worth*
A powerfully moving handbook that all women should read to reinforce their sense of female power.

TAPES
Jerry and Ester Hicks, *The Abraham-Hicks Tapes*
These tapes set out some very logical ideas about the laws of the universe. They helped me get through some trying times and inspired me to reaffirm that we alone have control over what happens to us. There is also a great website with articles and a monthly newsletter: www.abraham-hicks.com.

These courses have all profoundly affected my life.

Insight – Opening the Heart
Insight Seminars, Tel. +44 (0) 20 8883 2888;
e-mail: london@insight-seminars.org.uk; also available in America, Australia
and many other parts of the world.

If you have unhealed relationships or are inclined to be a bit of a victim,
this course offers a safe place to really become aware of limiting behaviour and
begin the healing. A great beginner's personal development course.

McKenna Breen, *NLP Practitioner course*
McKenna Breen Limited; Tel: +44 (0) 20 7704 6604; www.mckenna-breen.com
The only UK NLP Practitioner course featuring the originator of NLP, Richard
Bandler, one of my greatest teachers. Seven days of learning and *fun*. Many of
my clients have attended these courses on my recommendation and have really
expanded and enhanced what they have learnt from me.

Joseph Riggio, *The MythoSelf™ series*
www.appliednlp.com
The course where I learned to be at my best and live from there – highly
recommended if you want very powerful personal change. I am still one of
Joseph Riggio's students and I continue to learn more and more as I work with
him. Courses are held in the USA and UK.

OTHER RECOMMENDED BOOKS AND COURSES
RELATIONSHIPS
Books
David M. Buss, *The Evolution of Desire*, Basic Books
An in-depth study of human mating behaviour. Explains a lot!

Helen Fisher, *Anatomy of Love,* Fawcett Columbine
A cross-cultural study of marriage, mating, flirting, sex, adultery and more –
very enlightening.

Bradley Gerstman, Christopher Pizzo and Rich Seldes, *What Men Want*, HarperCollins

An interesting insight into three 30-something American male yuppies' ideas of how women should be.

Lillian Glass, *Attracting Terrific People*
A great little workbook for helping uncover your best you.

Gay and Kathlyn Hendricks, *Conscious Loving*, Bantam
How to move your relationship from co-dependence to co-commitment. A sensitively written workbook for couples, bursting with great ideas.

Susan Jeffers, *Opening our Hearts to Men*
How to avoid dependency.

Daphne Rose Kingma, *The Future of Love*, Broadway Books
Kingma explores where relationships have gone wrong and offers a more spiritual path to creating loving relationships in the 21st century.

Leil Lowndes, *How to Make Anyone Fall in Love with You* and *How to Talk to Anyone*, Thorsons
Great technique books, once you get the attitude and state of mind.

Web Resources

1,000 Questions for Couples
http://www.questionsforcouples.com
An interesting list of questions that can help you learn more about your partner *and* yourself.

SEXUALITY AND TANTRIC SEX

Books

The Barefoot Doctor, *The Barefoot Doctor's Handbook for Modern Lovers,* Piatkus
An amusing read and some useful ideas.

Mantak Chia, *Taoist Secrets of Love: Cultivating Male Sexual Energy,* Aurora Press
How men can go at it for hours and have multiple orgasms!

Mantak Chia and Douglas Abrams Arava, *The Multi-Orgasmic Man,* Thorsons
This is an ideal beginner's book on tantric sex. Its gentle introduction and focus on male needs is great for getting a man to explore this stuff. Give it as a present – it could change your sex life forever!

Richard Craze, *Tantric Sexuality: A Beginner's Guide*
I love this book. It's lighthearted and offers a simple intro to the basics of tantric sex without too much emphasis on the esoteric side.

Julia Henderson, *The Lover Within*
This is a superb little workbook for developing your sexual energy and enhancing your sexual ecstasy. I recommend it as an easy beginner's guidebook.

Phillip Hodson and Anne Hooper, *How to Make Great Love to a Man* and *How to Make Great Love to a Woman,* Robson Books
Two beautifully illustrated glossy hardback books which offer comprehensive information on every aspect of lovemaking from straight sex to whatever takes your fancy. Highly recommended.

Anne Moir and David Jessel, *Brain Sex,* Mandarin
Psychological, biological and genetic research into the stark difference between the male and female brains. A revolutionary book that helps to explain the male/female divide.

Courses

Diamond Light Tantra, *Tantra for Life*

www.diamondlighttantra.com

Leora Lightwoman runs splendid workshops on tantric sex, from introductory evenings to year-long courses. She facilitates the classes in the UK with her husband and tantric partner, Roger, a holistic doctor.

SPIRITUALITY – BEING THE BEST YOU ARE

Books

Renee Beck and Sydney Barbara Merrick, *The Art of Ritual*, Celestial Arts
A beautiful book for creating ritual anywhere, anytime.

Thom Hartmann, *The Greatest Spiritual Secret of the Century*,
www.thomhartmann.com
A wonderful parable explaining simple spiritual concepts.

Carolyn Myss, *Anatomy of the Spirit*
The seven stages of power and healing.

Carolyn Myss, *Sacred Contracts*, Harmony Books
A very comprehensive book on the roles people play including a powerful process that will help you to piece together the unique purpose of your life.

Robert Anton Wilson, *Prometheus Rising*, New Falcon Books
This book goes a long way to explaining and dissecting the ways in which humans have been programmed. It will challenge many of your ideas and turn you inside-out. Don't read this book if you aren't prepared to be well and truly shocked out of traditional ways of thinking!

Gary Zukav and Linda Francis, *The Heart of the Soul*, Simon & Schuster
If you want to know more about how your emotions affect you, this book is really helpful and healing.

ENERGY WORK

Books

David Carradine and Nakahara, *David Carradine's Introduction to Chi Kung*, Owl Books

An easy and slowly progressive programme to developing chi kung as a daily spiritual and physical practice. Includes healing and clearing exercises, with illustrations.

Videos/Tapes

The Heron School of Healing Arts, *An Introduction to Chi Kung*

Tel: 01323 647770 in the UK; available by mail order only

If you want to learn chi kung and work on healing your energy centres, this video by my teacher Peter Hudson is fantastic. Filmed to the background of the sea and the South Downs of England, it is simple and easy to follow. Learning chi kung changed my life in many powerful ways and it's easy to do on a regular basis.

Gabrielle Roth, *Endless Wave*

This tape offers a perfect meditation for those who are very touchy feely and active. I often recommend it to my clients as a way of helping them to express themselves more fully and access their sexual energy centres. Available through amazon.com or amazon.co.uk.

MEDITATION AND VISUALIZATION

Books

Shakti Gawain, *Creative Visualisation*

Simple and beautiful. The best book on visualization that I've ever read!

Dina Glouberman, *Life Choices, Life Changes*

Develop your personal vision with imagework. The book includes chapters such as 'Using the Past Creatively', and 'Making Life Decisions'.

Helen Graham, *Visualisation: An Introductory Guide*
Use visualization to improve your health and develop your self-awareness and creativity.

Christopher Hyatt, *Undoing Yourself with Energised Meditations*, New Falcon
Read it if you dare. This book is not mainstream, but it has some challenging ideas and bizarre methods of shaking yourself up.

DOING WHAT YOU LOVE AND LOVING WHAT YOU DO
Books
Richard N. Bolles, *What Colour is your Parachute?*
This book is fantastic and is updated yearly. It offers lots of resources, mainly American, but may have changed. It's great for uncovering what you love doing and are good at doing and how to go about starting it.

Barbara Sher, *I Could Do Anything, If Only I Knew What It Was* and *Live the Life You Love*
Barbara's books truly inspired me. They are well worth a read if you want to make a big change and do something you've always wanted to.

INFLUENCE AND PERSUASION AND LANGUAGE
Books
Tony Buzan, *Social Intelligence*, HarperCollins
A superb little book on how to become a more socially confident person.

Robert B. Cialdini, PhD, *Influence: The Psychology of Persuasion*, Quill
A fab book on the structure and background of influence. A must for all interested in the art of persuasion!

Alan Garner, *Conversationally Speaking*, Lowell House
A great introductory book which will guide you through the specifics of making conversation.

James Lawley and Penny Tompkins, *Metaphors in Mind: Transformation through Symbolic Modelling*
A fascinating book on how your metaphors and symbols can be used for personal transformation.

Deborah Tannen, *You Just Don't Understand: Women and Men in Conversation*, Virago, 1992
A discussion of the ways in which women and men use language differently. Useful for improving male/female conversation.

CDs and Tapes

Kenrick Cleveland, *MaxPersuasion 2000*
www.maxpersuasion.com
Cleveland is a master of persuasion and this is a really good CD series.

GENERAL PERSONAL DEVELOPMENT

Courses

Outlook Training Seminars
Tel: + 44 (0) 20 8905 5014; e-mail: outlooktrg@aol.com
An extremely powerful and enlightening personal development training series in which you access and experience your particular essence. Unbelievably empowering.

Books

Robin Chandler and Jo Ellen Grzyb, *The Nice Factor Book*, Simon & Schuster
How to put your needs first and not live a life of wanting to be liked by everyone.

Victor Frankl, *Man's Search for Meaning*
This book is inspiring. If you ever feel like giving up, read this – it'll put things in perspective.

Harriet Goldhor Lerner, *Dance of Anger*, *Dance of Intimacy* and *Dance of Deception*
These are totally brilliant self-development books. Written for women, but I recommend them to men as well.

Napoleon Hill, *Think and Grow Rich*
A huge success as a book and business, based on the power of self-belief.

Spencer Johnson, *Who Moved My Cheese?: An Amazing Way to Deal with Change in your Work and in your Life*
This book should be compulsory for life's 'victims'.

Joseph O'Connor and John Seymour, *Introducing Neuro Linguistic Programming*
This is the first book I ever read on NLP, the psychology behind much of what you have been learning in this book. It's a great beginner's book, but if you are interested it's wiser to take a course!

INTERNET DATING AND NETWORKING SITES

UK

www.buddynetwork.com A British interent site with an arena to network for professional and friendly purposes as well as comprehensive internet dating facilities. Buddy offers a unique in-depth profiling system which helps you discover who you are, what you want and how to present yourself in the best light.

www.singleagain.co.uk A first stop for anyone who is newly single. Regular magazine and advice on finance, friendships, home, children and more, with links to dating sites.

www.naturalfriends.co.uk An internet dating site for ecologically conscious non-smokers.

www.loveandfriends.com UK online dating agency associated with *Dancing Down the Moon.*

www.match.com A good starting-point to test out internet dating. Several of my friends have found romance on match.

PETA HESKELL
AND THE FLIRTING ACADEMY

Flirting Academy website: www.flirtcoach.com

Flirting Academy telephone: +44 (0) 700 4 354 784

COURSES

Flirting Weekend playshop – for singles and couples

Successfully Single days – how to be single and love it

Relationship Booster days – for couples who want to explore more about each other and their relationship

For more information call or e-mail courses@flirtcoach.com

COACHING PROGRAMMES

I offer a comprehensive singles and couples relationship-coaching programme including personal empowerment and couple mediation sessions and relationship contract facilitation. Individual coaching takes place via personal face-to-face sessions or over the telephone. Couple mediation and relationship-contract facilitation is only offered in face-to-face sessions.

For further information call or e-mail coaching@flirtcoach.com

INTERNATIONAL COURSE PROMOTION

If you are interested in sponsoring one of our courses in your country, please call or e-mail us for a preliminary discussion: international@flirtcoach.com

CORPORATE COURSES

The Flirting Academy also offers corporate charisma courses and after-dinner speeches. For more information, please call the Flirting Academy on +44 (0) 700 4 354 784 or e-mail corporate@flirtcoach.com

WEBSITE

Check out my constantly updated website which is packed full of articles on a variety of subjects, tips, solutions to problems, e-mail newsletter access, success stories, sexual humour, workshop details and links to flirting, sexuality and personal development sites, plus all the latest news
www.flirtingacademy.com

FEEDBACK

I can be contacted via this e-mail number. Please feel free to write to me with any comments or questions about this book. I will do my best to ensure all electronic correspondence receives a reply
feedback@flirtcoach.com

FLIRT COACH

PETA HESKELL

Communication Tips for Friendship, Love and Professional Success

Peta Heskell offers the key to magical communication, creating an energizing program to help you to be yourself at your best and love it. She encourages you to see flirting as a natural life skill to use, not just in romantic relationships, but in every human interaction to make communication more personalized, more influential and more fun!

Her dynamic and innovative action plan includes:

Looking inside – discover the real you and learn to revive your innate sense of child-like self-belief, curiosity, intuition and daring.

The outside – learn how to 'glow', become supersensitive to other people's signals, get your message across and attract the right people in your life.